THE IMITATION OF CHRIST

In Four Books

Thomas à Kempis

CONTENTS

THE IMITATION OF CHRIST
BOOK I.

BOOK II.

BOOK III.

BOOK IV.

THE IMITATION OF CHRIST.

BOOK I.

CHAPTER I.
OF FOLLOWING CHRIST, AND DESPISING ALL THE VANITIES OF THE WORLD.

1. *He that followeth me, walketh not in darkness,* saith our Lord, *John viii.* 12. These are the words of Christ, by which we are admonished that we must imitate his life and manners, if we would be truly enlightened, and delivered from all blindness of heart.

Let it then be our chief study to meditate on the life of Jesus Christ.

2. The doctrine of Christ surpasseth all the doctrines of the saints: and whosoever hath the Spirit, will find therein a hidden manna.

But it happeneth that many, by frequent hearing the gospel, are very little affected: because they have not the Spirit of Christ.

But he who would fully and feelingly understand the words of Christ: must study to make his whole life conformable to that of Christ.

3. What doth it avail thee, to discourse profoundly of the Trinity: if thou be void of humility, and consequently displeasing to the Trinity?

In truth, sublime words make not a man holy and just: but a virtuous life maketh him dear to God.

I had rather feel compunction, than know its definition.

If thou didst know the whole bible by heart, and the sayings of all the philosophers: what would it all profit thee, without the love of God and his grace?

Vanity of vanities, and all is vanity, besides loving God, and serving him alone.

This is the highest wisdom: by despising the world, to tend to heavenly kingdoms.

4. It is vanity therefore to seek after riches which must perish, and to trust in them.

It is vanity also to be ambitious of honours, and to raise one's self to a high station.

It is vanity to follow the lusts of the flesh: and to desire that for which thou must afterwards be grievously punished.

It is vanity to wish for a long life: and to take little care of leading a good life.

It is vanity to mind only this present life, and not to look forward into those things which are to come.

It is vanity to love that which passeth with all speed: and not to hasten thither where everlasting joy remains.

5. Often remember that proverb: The eye in not satisfied with seeing, nor is the ear filled with hearing. Ecclesiastes i. 8.

Study therefore to withdraw thy heart from the love of visible things, and to turn thyself to things invisible; For they that follow their sensuality, defile their conscience, and lose the grace of God.

CHAPTER II.
OF HAVING AN HUMBLE SENTIMENT OF ONE'S SELF.

1. All men naturally desire to know; but what doth knowledge avail without the fear of God?

Indeed an humble husbandman, that serveth God; is better than a proud philosopher, who, neglecting himself, considers the course of the heavens.

He, who knows himself well, is mean in his own eyes, and is not delighted with being praised by men.

If I should know all things that are in the world, and should not be in charity: what help would it be to me in the sight of God, who will judge me by my deeds?

2. Leave off that excessive desire of knowing: because there is found therein much distraction and deceit.

They who are learned, are desirous to appear and to be called wise.

There are many things, the knowledge of which is of little or no profit to the soul.

And he is very unwise who attends to other things than what may serve to his salvation.

Many words do not satisfy the soul; but a good life gives ease to the mind; and a pure conscience affords a great confidence in God.

3. The more and better thou knowest, the more heavy will be thy judgment, unless thy life be also more holy.

Be not therefore puffed up with any art or science; but rather fear upon account of the knowledge which is given thee.

If it seems to thee that thou knowest many things, and understandest them well enough: know at the same time that there are many more things of which thou art ignorant.

Be not high minded, but rather acknowledge thy ignorance.

Why wouldst thou prefer thyself to any one, since there are many more learned and skilful in the law than thyself?

If thou wouldst know and learn any thing to the purpose: love to be unknown, and esteemed as nothing.

4. This is the highest and most profitable lesson, truly to know, and to despise ourselves.

To have no opinion of ourselves, and to think always well and commendably of others, is great wisdom and high perfection.

If thou shouldst see another openly sin, or commit some heinous crime, yet thou oughtest not to esteem thyself better: because thou knowest not how long thou mayest remain in a good state.

We are all frail: but see thou think no one more frail than thyself.

CHAPTER III.
OF THE DOCTRINE OF TRUTH.

1. Happy is he whom *truth* teacheth by itself, not by figures and words that pass, but as it is in itself.

Our opinion, and our sense, often deceive us, and discover but little.

What signifies making a great dispute about abstruse and obscure matters, for not knowing of which we shall not be questioned at the day of judgment.

It is a great folly for us to neglect things profitable and necessary, and willingly to busy ourselves about those which are curious and hurtful.—We have eyes and see not.

2. And what need we concern ourselves about questions of philosophy?

He to whom the *Eternal Word* speaketh, is set at liberty from a multitude of opinions.

From *one Word* are all things, and this one all things speak: and this is *the beginning which also speaks to us*, John viii. 23.

Without this *Word* no one understands or judges rightly.

He to whom all things are *one* [Footnote], and who draws all things to *one*,—and who sees all things in *one*,—may be steady in heart, and peaceably repose in God.

> [Footnote: The Author seems here to allude to that passage of St. Paul, 1 Corinthians ii. 2. where he says, "That he desired to know nothing but Jesus Christ, and him crucified."]

O *Truth*, my God, make me one with thee in everlasting love.

I am weary with often reading and hearing many things: in thee is *all* that I will or desire.

Let all teachers hold their peace; let all creatures be silent in thy sight: speak thou alone to me.

3. The more a man is united within himself, and interiorly simple, the more and higher things doth he understand without labour: because he receives the light of understanding from above.

A pure, simple, and steady spirit, is not dissipated by a multitude of affairs; because he performs them all to the honour of God, and endeavours to be at rest within himself, and free from all seeking of himself.

Who is a greater hinderance and trouble to thee, than thine own unmortified affection of heart?

A good and devout man first disposes his works inwardly, which he is to do outwardly.

Neither do they draw him to the desires of an inordinate inclination: but he bends them to the rule of right reason.

Who has a stronger conflict than he who strives to overcome himself?

And this must be our business, to strive to overcome ourselves, and daily to gain strength against ourselves, and to grow better and better.

4. All perfections in this life are attended with some imperfections: and all our speculations with a certain obscurity.

The humble knowledge of thyself is a surer way to God, than the deepest search after science.

Learning is not to be blamed, nor the mere knowledge of any thing, which is good in itself, and ordained by God: but a good conscience and a virtuous life is always to be preferred before it.

But because many make it more their study to know, than to live well: therefore are they often deceived, and bring forth none, or very little fruit.

5. Oh! if men would use as much diligence in rooting out vices and planting virtues, as they do in proposing questions: there would not be so great evils committed, nor scandals among the people, nor so much relaxation in monasteries.

Verily, when the day of judgment comes, we shall not be examined what we have read, but what we have done; nor how learnedly we have spoken, but how religiously we have lived.

Tell me now where are all those great doctors, with whom thou wast well acquainted, whilst they were living, and flourished in learning?

Now others possess their livings, and I know not whether they ever think of them.

In their life-time they seemed to be something: and now they are not spoken of.

6. Oh! how quickly doth the glory of the world pass away! Would to God their lives had been answerable to their learning! then would they have studied and read well.

How many perish in the world thro' vain learning, who take little care of the service of God.

And because they chuse rather to be great than to be humble, therefore they are lost in their own imaginations.

He is truly great, who is great in charity.

He is truly great, who is little in his own eyes: and makes no account of the height of honour.

He is truly prudent, who looks upon all earthly things as dung, that he may gain Christ.

And he is very learned indeed, who does the will of God, and renounces his own will.

CHAPTER IV.
OF PRUDENCE IN OUR DOINGS.

1. We must not be easy in giving credit to every word or suggestion; but carefully and leisurely weigh the matter according to God.

Alas! such is our weakness, that we often more readily believe and speak of another that which is evil: than that which is good.

But perfect men do not easily give credit to every report; because they know man's weakness, which is very prone to evil, and very subject to fail in words.

2. It is great wisdom not to be rash in our doings: nor to maintain too obstinately our own opinion.

As also not to believe every man's word; nor presently to tell others the things which we have heard or believed.

Consult with the wise and conscientious man: and seek rather to be instructed by one that is better, than to follow thine own inventions.

A good life make's a man wise according to God, and expert in many things. The more humble a man is in himself, and more subject to God: the more wise will he be in all things, and the more at peace.

CHAPTER V.
OF READING THE HOLY SCRIPTURES.

1. Truth is to be sought for in holy scripture, not eloquence. All holy scripture ought to be read with that spirit with which it was made.

We must rather seek for profit in the scriptures, than for subtlety of speech.

We ought as willingly to read devout and simple books: as those that are high and profound.

Let not the authority of the writer offend thee, whether he was of little or great learning: but let the love of pure truth lead thee to read.

Enquire not who said this: but attend to what is said.

2. Men pass away: but the truth of the Lord remains for ever.

God speaks many ways to us: without respect of persons.

Our curiosity often hinders us in reading the scriptures, when we attempt to understand and discuss that which should be simply passed over.

If thou wilt receive profit, read with humility, simplicity, and faith: and seek not at any time the fame of being learned.

Willingly enquire after and hear with silence the words of the saints: and be pleased with the parables of the ancients: for they are not spoken without cause.

CHAPTER VI.
OF INORDINATE AFFECTION.

1. Whensoever a man desires any thing inordinately, he is presently disquieted within himself.

The proud and covetous are never easy.

The poor and humble of spirit, live in much peace.

The man that is not yet perfectly dead to himself, is soon tempted and overcome with small and trifling things.

He that is weak in spirit, and in a manner yet carnal and inclined to sensible things, can hardly withdraw himself wholly from earthly desires.

And therefore he is often sad, when he withdraws himself from them: and is easily moved to anger if any one thwarts him.

2. And if he has pursued his inclinations, he is presently tormented with the guilt of his conscience: because he has followed his passion, which helps him not at all towards the peace he sought for.

It is then by resisting our passions, that we are to find true peace of heart, and not by being slaves to them.

There is no peace therefore in the heart of a *carnal* man, nor in a man that is addicted to outward things: but only in a fervent spiritual man.

CHAPTER VII.
OF FLYING VAIN HOPE AND PRIDE.

1. He is vain who puts his trust in men, or in creatures.

Be not ashamed to serve others, and to appear poor in the world, for the love of Jesus Christ.

Confide not in thyself: but place thy hope in God.

Do what is in thy power, and God will be with thy good will.

Trust not in thy own knowledge, nor in the cunning of any man living: but rather in the grace of God, who helps the humble, and humbles those who presume of themselves.

2. Glory not in riches, if thou hast them; nor in friends, because they are powerful; but in God, who gives all things, and desires to give himself above all things.

Boast not of thy stature, nor beauty of the body, which is spoiled and disfigured by a little sickness.

Do not take a pride in thy talents or thy wit, lest thou displease God, to whom appertaineth every natural good quality and talent which thou hast.

3. Esteem not thyself better than others, lest perhaps thou be accounted worse in the sight of God, who knows what is in man.

Be not proud of thy own works: for the judgments of God are different from the judgments of men; and oftentimes, that displeaseth him, which pleaseth men.

If thou hast any thing of good, believe better things of others, that thou mayest preserve humility.

It will do thee no harm to esteem thyself the worst of all: but it will hurt thee very much to prefer thyself before any one.

Continual peace is with the humble: but in the heart of the proud, is frequent envy and indignation.

CHAPTER VIII.
OF SHUNNING TOO MUCH FAMILIARITY.

1. *Discover not thy heart to every one* (Ecclesiastes viii.): but treat of thy affairs with a man that is wise and feareth God.

Keep not much company with young people and strangers.

He not a flatterer with the rich: nor willingly appear before the great.

Associate thyself with the humble and simple, with the devout and virtuous: and treat of those things which may be to edification.

Be not familiar with any woman: but recommend all good women in general to God.

Desire to be familiar only with God and his angels: and fly the acquaintance of men.

We must have charity for all, but familiarity is not expedient.

It sometimes happens that a person, when not known, shines by a good reputation; who, when he is present, is disagreeable to them that see him.

We think sometimes to please others by being with them: and we begin rather to disgust them by the evil behaviour which they discover in us.

CHAPTER IX.
OF OBEDIENCE AND SUBJECTION.

1. It is a very great thing to stand in obedience, to live under a superior, and not to be at our own disposal.

It is much more secure to be in the state of subjection; than in authority.

Many are under obedience more out of necessity, than for the love of God: and such as these are in pain, and easily repine.

Nor will they gain freedom of mind, unless they submit themselves with their whole heart for God's sake.

Run here or there, thou will find no rest, but in an humble subjection under the government of a superior.

The imagination and changing of places has deceived many.

2. It is true, every one is desirous of acting according to his own liking; and is more inclined to such as are of his own mind.

But if God be amongst us, we must sometimes give up our own opinion for the sake of peace.

Who is so wise as to be able fully to know all things?

Therefore trust not too much to thine own thoughts: but be willing also to hear the sentiments of others.

Although thy opinion be good, yet if for God's sake thou leavest it, to follow that of another, it will be more profitable to thee.

3. For I have often heard, that it is more safe to hear and take counsel, than to give it.

It may also happen, that each one's thought may be good; but to refuse to yield to others, when reason or a just cause requires it, is a sign of pride and wilfulness.

CHAPTER X.
OF AVOIDING SUPERFLUITY OF WORDS.

1. Fly the tumult of men as much as thou canst: for treating of worldly affairs hinders very much, although they be discoursed of with a simple intention.

For we are quickly denied and ensnared with vanity.

I could wish I had often been silent, and that I had not been in company.

But why are we so willing to talk and discourse with one another: since we seldom return to silence without prejudice to our conscience?

The reason why we are so willing to talk, is, because by discoursing together we seek comfort from one another; and would gladly ease the heart, wearied by various thoughts.

And we very willingly talk and think of such things as we most love and desire, or which we imagine contrary to us.

2. But, alas! it is often in vain and to no purpose: for this outward consolation is no small hinderance of interior and divine comfort.

Therefore we must watch and pray, that our time may not pass away without fruit.

If it be lawful and expedient to speak, speak those things which may edify.

A bad custom and the neglect of our spiritual advancement, is a great cause of our keeping so little guard upon our mouth.

But devout conferences concerning spiritual things, help very much to spiritual progress: especially where persons of the same mind and spirit are associated together in God.

CHAPTER XI.
OF ACQUIRING PEACE AND ZEAL OF SPIRITUAL PROGRESS.

1. We might have much peace, if we would not busy ourselves with the sayings and doings of others, and with things which belong not to us.

How can he remain long in peace, who entangles himself with other people's cares; who seeks occasions abroad, and who is little or seldom inwardly recollected?

Blessed are the single hearted, for they shall enjoy much peace.

2. What was the reason why some of the saints were so perfect and contemplative?

Because they made it their study wholly to mortify in themselves all earthly desires; and thus they were enabled, with the whole interior of their hearts, to cleave to God, and freely to attend to themselves.

We are too much taken up with our own passions; and too solicitous about transitory things.

And seldom do we perfectly overcome so much as one vice, nor are we earnestly bent upon our daily progress; and therefore we remain cold and tepid.

3. If we were perfectly dead to ourselves and no ways entangled in our interior: then might we be able to relish things divine, and experience something of heavenly contemplation.

The whole and greatest hinderance is, because we are not free from passions and lusts; nor do we strive to walk in the perfect way of the saints.

And when we meet with any small adversity, we are too quickly dejected, and turn away to seek after human consolation.

4. If we strove like valiant men to stand in the battle; doubtless we should see that our Lord would help us from heaven.

For he is ready to help them that fight and trust in his grace: who furnishes us with occasions of fighting that we may overcome.

If we place our progress in religion in these outward observances only, our devotion will quickly be at an end.

But let us lay the axe to the root, that being purged from passions, we may possess a quiet mind.

5. If every year we rooted out one vice, we should soon become perfect men.

But now we often find it quite otherwise: that we were better and more pure in the beginning of our conversion, than after many years of our profession.

Our fervour and progress ought to be every day greater: but now it is esteemed a great matter if a man can retain some part of his first fervour.

If we could use but a little violence upon ourselves in the beginning, we might afterwards do all things with ease and joy.

It is hard to leave off our old customs: and harder to go against our own will.

But if thou dost not overcome things that are small and light: when wilt thou overcome greater difficulties?

Resist thy inclination in the beginning, and break off the evil habit; lest perhaps by little and little the difficulty increase upon thee.

O! if thou wert sensible how much peace thou shouldst procure to thyself, and joy to others, by behaving thyself well; thou wouldst be more solicitous for thy spiritual progress.

CHAPTER XII.
OF THE ADVANTAGE OF ADVERSITY.

1. It is good for us to have sometimes troubles and adversities; for they make a man enter into himself, that he may know that he is in a state of banishment, and may not place his hopes in any thing of this world.

It is good that we sometimes suffer contradictions, and that men have an evil or imperfect opinion of us; even when we do and intend well.

These things are often helps to humility, and defend us from vain glory.

For then we better run to God our inward witness, when outwardly we are despised by men, and little credit is given to us.

2. Therefore should a man establish himself in such a manner in God, as to have no need of seeking many comforts from men.

When a ***man of good will*** is troubled or tempted, or afflicted with evil thoughts; then he better understands what need he hath of God, without whom he finds he can do no good.

Then also he laments; he sighs, and prays by reason of the miseries which he suffers.

Then he is weary of living longer: and wishes death to come that he may be ***dissolved and be with Christ***.

Then also he well perceives that perfect security and full peace cannot be found in this world.

CHAPTER XIII.
OF RESISTING TEMPTATION.

1. As long as we live in this world, we cannot be without tribulation and temptation.

Hence it is written in Job: Man's life upon earth is a temptation.

Therefore ought every one to be solicitous about his temptations, and to watch in prayer; lest the devil, (who never sleeps, but ***goes about seeking whom he may devour***,) find room to deceive him.

No man is so perfect and holy as not to have sometimes temptations: and we cannot be wholly without them.

2. Temptations are often very profitable to a man, although they be troublesome and grievous: for in them a man is humbled, purified, and instructed.

All the saints have passed through many tribulations and temptations, and have profited by them: and they who could not support temptations, have become reprobates, and fell off.

There is not any order so holy, nor place so retired, where there are not temptations and adversities.

3. A man is never entirely secure from temptations as long as he lives: because we have within us the source of temptations, having been born in concupiscence.

When one temptation or tribulation is over, another comes on: and we shall have always something to suffer, because we have lost the good of our original happiness.

Many seek to fly temptations, and fall more grievously into them.

By flight alone we cannot overcome: but by patience and true humility we are made stronger than all our enemies.

4. He that only declines them outwardly, and does not pluck out the root, will profit little; nay, temptations will sooner return to him, and he will find himself in a worse condition.

By degrees, and by patience, with longanimity, thou shalt, by God's grace, better overcome them, than by harshness and thine own importunity.

In temptation, often take counsel, and deal not roughly with one that is tempted: but comfort him, as thou wouldst wish to be done to thyself.

5. Inconstancy of mind, and small confidence in God, is the beginning of all temptations.

For as a ship without a rudder is tossed to and fro by the waves: so the man who is remiss, and who quits his resolution, is many ways tempted.

Fire tries iron, and temptation tries a just man.

We often know not what we can do: but temptation discovers what we are.

6. However, we must be watchful, especially in the beginning of temptation: because then the enemy is easier overcome, when he is not suffered to come in at the door of the soul, but is kept out and resisted at his first knock.

Whence a certain man said: Withstand the beginning, after-remedies come too late.

For first a bare thought comes to the mind, then a strong imagination; afterwards delight, and evil motion and consent.

And thus, by little and little, the wicked enemy gets full entrance, when he is not resisted in the beginning.

And how much the longer a man is negligent in resisting: so much the weaker does he daily become in himself, and the enemy becomes stronger against him.

7. Some suffer great temptations in the beginning of their conversion, and some in the end.

And some there are who are much troubled in a manner all their life time.

Some are but lightly tempted, according to the Wisdom and equity of the ordinance of God, who weighs the state and merits of men, and pre-ordains all for the salvation of his elect.

8. We must not therefore despair when we are tempted, but pray to God with so much the more fervour, that he may vouchsafe to help us in all tribulations: who, no doubt, according to the saying of St. Paul, will *make such issue with the temptation, that we may be able to sustain it.* 1 Corinthians x.

Let us therefore humble our souls, under the hand of God in all temptations and tribulations: for the humble in spirit he will save and exalt.

9. In temptations and tribulations, a man is proved what progress he has made: and in them there is greater merit, and his virtue appears more conspicuous.

Nor is it much if a man be devout and fervent when he feels no trouble: but if in the time of adversity he bears up with patience, there will be hope of a great advancement.

Some are preserved from great temptations, and are often overcome in daily little ones: that being humbled, they may never presume of themselves in great things, who are weak in such small occurrences.

CHAPTER XIV.
OF AVOIDING RASH JUDGMENT.

1. Turn thy eyes back upon thyself, and see thou judge not the doings of others.

In judging others a man labours in vain, often errs, and easily sins; but in judging and looking into himself, he always labours with fruit.

We frequently judge of a thing according as we have it at heart: for we easily love true judgment through private affection.

If God were always the only object of our desire, we should not so easily be disturbed at the resistance of our opinions.

2. But there is often something lies hid within, or occurs from without, which draws us along with it.

Many secretly seek themselves in what they do, and are not sensible of it.

They seem also to continue in good peace, when things are done according to their will and judgment: but if it fall out contrary to their desires, they are soon moved and become sad.

Difference of thoughts and opinions is too frequently the source of dissensions amongst friends and neighbours, amongst religious and devout persons.

3. An old custom is with difficulty relinquished: and no man is led willingly farther than himself sees or likes.

If thou reliest more upon thine own reason or industry than upon the virtue that subjects to Jesus Christ, thou wilt seldom and hardly be an *enlightened* man: for God will have us perfectly subject to himself, and to transcend all reason by inflamed love.

CHAPTER XV.
OF WORKS DONE OUT OF CHARITY.

1. Evil ought not to be done, either for any thing in the world, or for the love of any man: but for the profit of one that stands in need, a good work is sometimes freely to be omitted, or rather to be changed for a better.

For, by doing thus, a good work is not lost, but is changed into a better.

Without charity, the outward work profiteth nothing: but whatever is done out of charity, be it ever so little and contemptible, all becomes fruitful.

For God regards more with how much affection and love a person performs a work, than how much he does.

2. He does much who loves much.

He does much that does well what he does.

He does well who regards rather the common good than his own will.

That seems often to be charity which is rather natural affection: because our own natural inclination, self-will, hope of retribution, desire of our own interest, will seldom be wanting.

3. He that has true and perfect charity, seeks himself in no one thing: but desires only the glory of God in all things.

He envies no man, because he loves no private joy; nor does he desire to rejoice in himself: but above all good things, he wishes to be made happy in God.

He attributes nothing of good in any man, but refers it totally to God, from whom all things proceed as from their fountain, in the enjoyment of whom all the saints repose as in their last end.

Ah! if a man had but one spark of perfect charity, he would doubtless perceive that all earthly things are full of vanity.

CHAPTER XVI.
OF BEARING THE DEFECTS OF OTHERS.

1. What a man cannot amend in himself or others, he must bear with patience, till God ordains otherwise.

Think, that it perhaps is better so for thy trial and patience: without which, our merits are little worth.

Thou must, nevertheless, under such impressions, earnestly pray that God may vouchsafe to help thee, and that thou mayest bear them well.

2. If any one being once or twice admonished, does not comply, contend not with him: but commit all to God, that his will may be done, and he may be honoured in all his servants, who knows how to convert evil into good.

Endeavour to be patient in supporting others defects and infirmities of what kind so ever: because thou also hast many things which others must bear withal.

If thou canst not make thyself such a one as thou wouldst: how canst thou expect to have another according to thy liking?

We would willingly have others perfect: and yet we mend not, our own defects.

3. We would have others strictly corrected: but are not willing to be corrected ourselves.

The large liberty of others displeases us: and yet we would not be denied any thing we ask for.

We are willing that others should be bound up by laws: and we suffer not ourselves by any means to be restrained.

Thus it is evident how seldom we weigh our neighbour in the same balance with ourselves.

If all were perfect: what then should we have to suffer from others for God's sake?

4. But now God has so disposed things, that we may learn to bear one another's burdens: for there is no man without defect; no man without his burden: no man sufficient for himself; no man wise enough for himself: but we must support one another, comfort one another, assist, instruct, and admonish one another.

But how great each one's virtue is, best appears by occasion of adversity: for occasions do not make a man frail, but shew what he is.

CHAPTER XVII.
OF A MONASTIC LIFE.

1. Thou must learn to renounce thy own will in many things, if thou wilt keep peace and concord with others.

It is no small matter to live in a monastery, or in a congregation, and to converse therein without reproof, and to persevere faithful till death.

Blessed is he who has there lived well, and made a happy end.

If thou wilt stand as thou oughtest, and make a due progress, look upon thyself as a banished man, and a stranger upon earth.

Thou must be content to be made a fool for Christ, if thou wilt lead a religious life.

2. The habit and the tonsure contribute little; but a change of manners, and an entire mortification of the passions, make a true religious man.

He that seeks here any other thing than purely God and the salvation of his soul, will find nothing but trouble and sorrow.

Neither can he long remain in peace, who does not strive to be the least, and subject to all.

3. Thou camest hither to serve, not to govern: know that thou art called to suffer and to labour, not to be idle and talkative.

Here then men are tried as gold in the furnace.

Here no man can stand, unless he be willing with all his heart to humble himself for the love of God.

CHAPTER XVIII.
OF THE EXAMPLE OF THE HOLY FATHERS.

1. Look upon the lively examples of the holy fathers, in whom true perfection and religion was most shining, and thou wilt see how little, and almost nothing, that is which we do.

Alas! what is our life if compared to theirs?

The saints and friends of Christ served the Lord in hunger and thirst; in cold and nakedness; in labour and weariness; in watchings and fastings; in prayers and holy meditations; in persecutions and many reproaches.

2. Ah! how many and how grievous tribulations have the apostles, martyrs, confessors, virgins, and all the rest, gone through, who have been willing to follow Christ's footsteps: for they hated their lives in this world, that they might possess them for eternity.

O! how strict and mortified a life did the holy fathers lead in the desert! How long and grievous temptations did they endure! how often were they molested by the enemy! What frequent and fervent prayers did they offer to God! What rigorous abstinence did they go through! What great zeal and fervour had they for their spiritual progress! How strong a war did they wage for overcoming vice! How pure and upright was their intention to God!

They laboured all the day, and in the nights, they gave themselves to long prayers: though even whilst they were at work, they ceased not from mental prayer.

3. They spent all their time profitably: every hour seemed short which they spent with God: and through the great sweetness of divine contemplation, they forgot even the necessity of their bodily refreshment.

They renounced all riches, dignities, honours, friends, and kindred; they desired to have nothing of this world; they scarce allowed themselves the necessaries of life: the serving the body even in necessity, was irksome to them.

They were poor, therefore, as to earthly things: but very rich in grace and virtues.

Outwardly they wanted, but inwardly they were refreshed with divine graces and consolations.

4. They were strangers to the world: but near and familiar friends to God.

They seemed to themselves as nothing, and were despised by this world: but in the eyes of God they were very valuable and beloved.

They stood in true humility, they lived in simple obedience, they walked in charity and patience: and therefore they daily advanced in spirit, and obtained great favour with God.

They were given as an example for all religious: and ought more to excite us to make good progress, than the number of the lukewarm to grow slack.

5. O! how great was the fervour of all religious in the beginning of their holy institution!

O! how great was their devotion in prayer! how great their zeal for virtue!

How great discipline was in force amongst them! How great reverence and obedience in all, flourished under the rule of a superior!

The footsteps remaining still bear witness that they were truly perfect and holy men: who waging war so stoutly, trod the world under their feet.

Now he is thought great who is not a transgressor: and who can with patience endure what he hath undertaken.

6. Ah! the lukewarmness and negligence of our state, that we so quickly fall away from our former fervour, and are now even weary of living through sloth and tepidity!

Would to God that advancement in virtues were not wholly asleep in thee, who hast often seen many examples of the devout!

CHAPTER XIX.
OF THE EXERCISES OF A GOOD RELIGIOUS MAN.

1. The life of a good religious man ought to be eminent in all virtue: that he may be such interiorly, as he appears to men in his exterior.

And with good reason ought he to be much more in his interior, than he exteriorly appears; because he who beholds us is God, of whom we ought exceedingly to stand in awe, wherever we are, and like angels walk pure in his sight.

We ought every day to renew our resolution, and excite ourselves to fervour, as if it were the first day of our conversion, and to say:

Help me, O Lord God, in my good resolution, and in thy holy service, and give me grace now this day perfectly to begin; for what I have hitherto done, is nothing.

2. According as our resolution is, will the progress of our advancement be; and he had need of much diligence who would advance much.

Now if he that makes a strong resolution often fails: what will he do who seldom or but weakly resolves?

The falling off from our resolution happens divers ways: and a small omission in our exercises seldom passeth without some loss.

The resolutions of the just depend on the grace of God, rather than on their own wisdom: and in whom they always put their trust, whatever they take in hand.

For man proposes, but God disposes: nor is the way of man in his own hands.

3. If for piety's sake, or with a design to the profit of our brother, we sometimes omit our accustomed exercises, it may afterwards be easily recovered.

But if through a loathing of mind, or negligence, it be lightly let alone, it is no small fault, and will prove hurtful.

Let us endeavour what we can, we shall still be apt to fail in many things.

But yet we must always resolve on something certain, and in particular against those things which hinder us most.

We must examine and order well both our exterior and interior! because both conduce to our advancement.

4. If thou canst not continually recollect thyself, do it sometimes, and at least once a day, that is, at morning or evening.

In the morning resolve, in the evening examine thy performances: how thou hast behaved this day in word, work, or thought: because in these perhaps thou hast often offended God and thy neighbour.

Prepare thyself like a man to resist the wicked attacks of the devil; bridle gluttony, and thou shalt the easier restrain all carnal inclinations.

Be never altogether idle: but either reading, or writing, or praying, or meditating, or labouring in something that may be for the common good.

Yet in bodily exercises, a discretion is to be used: nor are they equally to be undertaken by all.

5. Those things which are not *common* are not to be done in public: for *particular* things are more safely done in private.

But take care then be not slack in common exercises, and more forward in things of thy own particular devotion: but having fully, and faithfully performed what thou art bound to, and what is enjoined thee, if thou hast any time remaining, give thyself to thyself according as thy devotion shall incline thee.

All cannot have the self same exercise: but this is more proper for one, and that for another.

Moreover, according to the diversity of times, divers exercises are more pleasing: for some relish better on festival days, others on common days.

We stand in need of one kind in time of temptation, and of another in time of peace and rest.

Some we willingly think on when we are sad, others when we are joyful in the Lord.

6. About the time of the principal festivals, we must renew our good exercises: and more fervently implore the prayers of the saints.

We ought to make our resolution from festival to festival: as if we were then to depart out of this world, and to come to the everlasting festival.

Therefore we ought carefully to prepare ourselves at times of devotion; and to converse more devoutly, and keep all observances more strictly, as being shortly to receive the reward of our labour from God.

7. And if it be deferred, let us believe that we are not well prepared, and that we are as yet unworthy of the great glory which shall be revealed in us at the appointed time: and let us endeavour to prepare ourselves better for our departure.

Blessed is that servant, says the evangelist St. Luke, whom when his Lord shall come he shall find watching. Amen, I say to you, he shall set him over all his possessions. Luke xiii.

CHAPTER XX.
OF THE LOVE OF SOLITUDE AND SILENCE.

1. Seek a proper time to retire into thyself, and often think of the benefits of God.

Let curiosities alone.

Read such matters as may rather move thee to compunction, than give thee occupation.

If thou wilt withdraw thyself from superfluous talk and idle visits, as also from giving ear to news and reports, thou wilt find time sufficient and proper to employ thyself in good meditations.

The greatest saints avoided the company of men as much as they could, and chose to live to God in secret.

2. As often as I have been amongst men, said one, I have returned less a man: this we often experience when we talk long.

It is easier to be altogether silent, than not to exceed in words.

It is easier to keep retired at home, than to be able to be sufficiently upon one's guard abroad.

Whosoever, therefore, aims at arriving at *internal* and *spiritual* things, must, with Jesus, go aside from the crowd.

No man is secure in appearing abroad, but he who would willingly lie hid at home.

No man securely speaks, but he who loves to hold his peace.

No man securely governs, but he who would willingly live in subjection.

No man securely commands, but he who has learned well to obey.

3. No man securely rejoiceth, unless he has within him the testimony of a good conscience.

Yet the security of the saints was always full of the fear of God.

Neither were they less careful or humble in themselves because they were shining with great virtues and grace.

But the security of the wicked arises from pride and presumption; and will end in deceiving themselves.

Never promise thyself security in this life, though thou seemest to be a good religious man, or a devout hermit.

4. Oftentimes they that were better in the judgments of men, have been in greater danger by reason of their too great confidence.

So that it is better for many not to be altogether free from temptations, but to be often assaulted; that they may not be too secure: lest, perhaps, they be lifted up with pride, or take more liberty to go aside after exterior comforts.

O! how good a conscience would that man preserve, who would never seek after transitory joy, nor ever busy himself with the world.

O! how great peace and tranquillity would he possess, who would cut off all vain solicitude, and only think of the things of God and his salvation, and place his whole hope in God.

5. No man is worthy of heavenly comfort who has not diligently exercised himself in holy compunction.

If thou wouldst find compunction in thy heart, retire into thy chamber, and shut out the tumults of the world, as it is written: *Have compunction in your chambers*. Psalms iv.

Thou shalt find in thy cell what thou shalt often lose abroad.

Thy cell, if thou continue in it, grows sweet: but if thou keep not to it, it becomes tedious and distasteful.

If in the beginning of thy conversion thou accustom thyself to remain in thy cell, and keep it well; it will be to thee afterwards a dear friend, and a most agreeable delight.

6. In silence and quiet the devout soul goes forward, and learns the secrets of the scriptures.

There she finds floods of tears, with which she may wash and cleanse herself every night: that she may become so much the more familiar with her Maker, by how much the farther she lives from all worldly tumult.

For God with his holy angels will draw nigh to him, who withdraws himself from his acquaintance and friends.

It is better to lie hid, and take care of one's self, than neglecting one's self to work even miracles.

It is commendable for a religious man, to go seldom abroad, to fly being seen, and not to desire to see men.

7. Why wilt thou see what thou must not have? *The world passeth and its concupiscences*. 1 John ii.

The desires of sensuality draw thee abroad: but when the hour is past, what dost thou bring home, but a weight upon thy conscience, and a dissipation of heart.

A joyful going abroad often brings forth a sorrowful coming home, and a merry evening makes a sad morning.

So all carnal joy enters pleasantly; but in the end brings remorse and death.

What canst thou see elsewhere which thou seest not here? Behold the heaven and the earth, and all the elements; for of these are all things made.

8. What canst thou see any where which can continue long under the sun?

Thou thinkest perhaps to be satisfied, but thou canst not attain to it.

If thou couldst see any thing at once before thee, what would it be but a vain sight?

Lift up thine eyes to God on high, and pray for thy sins and negligences.

Leave vain things to vain people: but mind thou the things which God has commanded thee.

Shut thy doors upon thee, and call to thee Jesus thy beloved.

Stay with him in thy cell, for thou shalt not find so great peace any where else.

If thou hadst not gone abroad, and hearkened to rumours, thou hadst kept thyself better in good peace: but since thou art delighted sometimes to hear news, thou must from thence suffer a disturbance of heart.

CHAPTER XXI.
OF COMPUNCTION OF HEART.

1. If thou wilt make any progress keep thyself in the fear of God, and be not too free, but restrain all thy senses under discipline, and give not thyself up to foolish mirth.

Give thyself to compunction of heart, and thou shalt find devotion.

Compunction opens the way to much good, which dissolution is wont quickly to lose.

It is wonderful that any man can heartily rejoice in this life, who weighs and considers his banishment, and the many dangers of his soul.

2. Through levity of heart, and the little thought we have of our defects, we feel not the sorrows of our soul: but often vainly laugh, when in all reason we ought to weep.

There is no true liberty, nor good joy, but in the fear of God with a good conscience.

Happy is he who can cast away all impediments of distractions, and recollect himself to the union of holy communion.

Happy is he who separates himself from all that may burthen or defile his conscience.

Strive manfully: custom is overcome by custom.

If thou canst let men alone, they will let thee do what thou hast to do.

3. Busy not thyself with other men's affairs, nor entangle thyself with the causes of great ones.

Have always an eye upon thyself in the first place: and take special care to admonish thyself preferably to all thy dearest friends.

If thou hast not the favour of men, be not grieved thereat: but let thy concern be, that thou dost not carry thyself so well and so circumspectly as it becomes a servant of God, and a devout religious man to demean himself.

It is oftentimes more profitable and more secure for a man not to have many comforts in this life; especially according to the flesh.

Yet, that we have not divine comforts, or seldom experience them, is our own faults: because we do not seek compunction of heart, nor cast off altogether vain and outward satisfactions.

4. Acknowledge thyself unworthy of divine consolation, and rather worthy of much tribulation.

When a man has perfect compunction, then the whole world is to him burdensome and distasteful.

A good man always finds subject enough for mourning and weeping.

For whether he considers himself, or thinks of his neighbour, he knows that no man lives here without tribulations; and the more thoroughly he considers himself, the more he grieves.

The subjects for just grief and interior compunction are our vices and sins, in which we lie entangled in such manner, as seldom to be able to contemplate heavenly things.

5. If thou wouldst oftener think of thy death, than of a long life, no doubt but thou wouldst more fervently amend thyself.

And if thou didst seriously consider in thy heart the future punishments of hell and purgatory, I believe thou wouldst willingly endure labour and pain, and fear no kind of austerity.

But because these things reach not the heart, and we still love the things which flatter us, therefore we remain cold and very sluggish.

6. It is oftentimes a want of *spirit*, which makes the wretched body so easily complain.

Pray therefore humbly to our Lord, that he may give thee the spirit of compunction: and say with the prophet: *Feed me, Lord, with the food of tears, and give me drink of tears in measure*.

CHAPTER XXII.
OF THE CONSIDERATION OF THE MISERY OF MAN.

1. Thou art miserable wherever thou art, and which way soever thou turnest thyself, unless thou turn thyself to God.

Why art thou troubled because things do not succeed with thee according to thy will and desire?

Who is there that has all things according to his will?

Neither I, nor thou, nor any man upon earth.

There is no man in the world without some trouble or affliction, though he be a king or a pope.

Who is there that is most at ease? doubtless he who is willing to suffer something for God's sake.

2. Many unstable and weak men are apt to say: behold how well such a one lives, how rich, how great, how mighty and powerful!

But attend to heavenly goods, and thou wilt see that all these temporal things are nothing, but very uncertain, and rather burdensome: because they are never possessed without care and fear.

The happiness of a man consisteth not in having temporal things in abundance, but a moderate competency sufficeth.

It is truly a misery to live upon earth.

The more a man desireth to be spiritual, the more this present life becomes distasteful to him: because he the better understands, and more clearly sees the defects of human corruption.

For to eat, drink, watch, sleep, rest, labour, and to be subject to other necessities of nature, is truly a great misery and affliction to a devout man, who desires to be released, and free from all sin.

3. For the *inward* man is very much burdened with the necessities of the body in this world.

And therefore the prophet devoutly prays to be freed from them, saying: *From my necessities deliver me, O Lord*. Psalms xxiv.

But wo to them that know not their own misery, and more wo to them that love this miserable and corruptible life.

For some there are who love it to that degree, although they can scarce get necessaries by labouring or begging, that if they could live always here, they would not care at all for the kingdom of God.

4. O senseless people, and infidels in heart, who lie buried so deep in earthly things, as to relish nothing but the things of the flesh!

Miserable wretches! they will in the end find to their cost, how vile a nothing that was which they so much loved.

But the saints of God, and all the devout friends of Christ, made no account of what pleased the flesh, or flourished in this life; but their whole hope and intentions aspired to eternal goods.

Their whole desire tended upwards to things everlasting and invisible; for fear lest the love of visible things should draw them down to things below.

Lose not, brother, thy confidence of going forward to spiritual things; there is yet time, the hour is not yet past.

5. Why wilt thou put off thy resolution from day to day? Arise, and begin this very moment, and say: Now is the time for doing, and now is the time to fight; now is the proper time to amend my life.

When thou art troubled and afflicted, then is the time to merit.

Thou must pass through fire and water, before thou comest to refreshment.

Unless thou do violence to thyself, thou wilt not overcome vice.

As long as we carry about us this frail body, we cannot be without sin, nor live without uneasiness and sorrow.

We would fain be at rest from all misery: but because we have lost innocence by sin, we have also lost true happiness.

We must therefore have patience, and wait for the mercy of God, till iniquity pass away, and this mortality be swallowed up by immortal life.

6. O! how great is human frailty, which is always prone to vice!

To-day thou confessest thy sins, and to-morrow thou again committest what thou hast confessed!

Now thou resolvest to take care, and an hour after thou dost as if thou hadst never resolved.

We have reason therefore to humble ourselves, and never to think much of ourselves, since we are so frail and inconstant.

That may also quickly be lost through negligence, which with much labour and time was hardly gotten by grace.

7. What will become of us yet in the end: who grow lukewarm so very soon?

Wo be to us if we are for giving ourselves to rest, as if we had already met with peace and security, when there does not appear any mark of true sanctity in our conversation.

It would be very needful that we should yet again, like good novices, be instructed in all good behaviour: if so, perhaps there would be hopes of some future amendment, and greater spiritual progress.

CHAPTER XXIII.
OF THE THOUGHTS OF DEATH.

1. Very quickly must thou be gone from hence: see then how matters stand with thee: a man is here to-day, and to-morrow he is vanished.

And when he is taken away from the sight, he is quickly also out of mind.

O! the dulness and hardness of man's heart, which only thinks on what is present, and looks not forward to things to come!

Thou oughtest in every action and thought so to order thyself, as if thou wert immediately to die.

If thou hast a good conscience, thou wouldst not much fear death.

It were better for thee to fly sin, than to be afraid of death.

If thou art not prepared to-day, how wilt thou be to-morrow?

To-morrow is an uncertain day; and how dost thou know that thou shalt be alive to-morrow?

2. What benefit is it to live long, when we advance so little?

Ah! long life does not always make us better, but often adds to our guilt!

Would to God we had behaved ourselves well in this world, even for one day!

Many count the years of their conversion; but oftentimes the fruit of amendment is but small.

If it be frightful to die, perhaps it will be more dangerous to live longer.

Blessed is he that has always the hour of his death before his eyes, and every day disposes himself to die.

If thou hast at any time seen a man die, think that thou must also pass the same way.

3. In the morning, imagine thou shalt not live till night: and when evening comes, presume not to promise thyself the next morning.

Be therefore always prepared, and live in such a manner, that death may never find thee unprovided.

Many die suddenly, and when they little think of it: *For the Son of Man will come at the hour when he is not looked for*. Matthew xxiv. When that last hour shall come, thou wilt begin to have quite other thoughts of thy whole past life: and thou wilt be exceedingly grieved that thou hast been so negligent and remiss.

4. How happy and prudent is he who strives to be such now in this life, as he desires to be found at his death.

For it will give a man a great confidence of dying happily, if he has a perfect contempt of the world, a fervent desire of advancing in virtue, a love for discipline, the spirit of penance, a ready obedience, self-denial, and patience in bearing all adversities for the love of Christ.

Thou mayest do many good things whilst thou art well: but when thou art sick, I know not what thou wilt be able to do.

Few are improved by sickness; they also that travel much abroad seldom become holy.

5. Trust not in thy friends and kinsfolks, nor put off the welfare of thy soul to hereafter: for men will sooner forget thee than thou imaginest.

It is better now to provide in time and send some good before thee, than to trust to others helping thee after thy death.

If thou art not now careful for thyself, who will be careful for thee hereafter?

The present time is very precious: *Now are the days of salvation*: now is an acceptable time.

But it is greatly to be lamented, that thou dost not spend this time more profitably: wherein thou mayest acquire a stock on which thou mayest live for ever! The time will come, when thou wilt wish for one day or hour to amend: and I know not whether thou wilt obtain it.

6. O my dearly beloved, from how great a danger mayest thou deliver thyself: from how great a fear mayest thou be freed, if thou wilt but now be always fearful, and looking for death! Strive now so to live, that in the hour of thy death thou mayest rather rejoice than fear.

Learn now to die to the world, that then thou mayest begin to live with Christ.

Learn now to despise all things, that then thou mayest freely go to Christ.

Chastise thy body now by penance, that thou mayest then have an assured confidence.

7. Ah! fool! why dost thou think to live long, when thou art not sure of one day?

How many thinking to live long, have been deceived, and unexpectedly have been snatched away.

How often hast thou heard related, that such a one was slain by the sword; another drowned; another falling from on high, broke his neck: this man died at the table; that other came to his end when he was at play.

Some have perished by fire; some by the sword; some by pestilence; and some by robbers.

Thus death is the end of all, and man's life passeth suddenly like a shadow.

8. Who will remember thee when thou art dead; and who will pray for thee?

Do now, beloved, do now all thou canst, because thou knowest not when thou shalt die: nor dust thou know what shall befal thee after death.

Whilst thou hast time, heap up to thyself riches that will never die; think of nothing but thy salvation; care for nothing but the things of God.

Make now to thyself friends, by honouring the saints of God, and imitating their actions; that when thou shalt fail in this life, they may receive thee into everlasting dwellings.

9. Keep thyself as a pilgrim, and a stranger upon earth, to whom the affairs of this world do not in the least belong.

Keep thy heart free, and raised upwards to God; because thou hast not here a lasting city.

Send thither thy daily prayer, with sighs and tears; that after death thy spirit may be worthy to pass happily to our Lord. **Amen**.

CHAPTER XXIV.
OF JUDGMENT AND THE PUNISHMENT OF SINS.

1. In all things look to thy end, and how thou shalt be able to stand before a severe Judge, to whom nothing is hidden: who takes no bribes, nor receives excuses, but will judge that which is just.

O most wretched and foolish sinner, what answer wilt thou make to God, who knows all thy evils? thou who sometimes art afraid of the looks of an angry man.

Why dost thou not provide for thy self against the day of judgment, when no man can be excused or defended by another; but every one shall have enough to do to answer for himself?

At present thy labour is profitable; thy tears are acceptable; thy sighs will be heard, and thy sorrow is satisfactory, and may purge away thy sins.

2. A patient man hath a great and wholesome purgatory, who receiving injuries is more concerned at another person's sin than his own wrong; who willingly prays for his adversaries, and from his heart forgives offences; who delays not to ask forgiveness of others; who is easier moved to compassion than to anger; who frequently useth violence to himself, and labours to bring the flesh wholly under subjection to the spirit.

It is better now to purge away our sins, and cut up our vices, than to reserve them to be purged hereafter.

Truly, we deceive ourselves through the inordinate love we bear to our flesh.

3. What other things shall that fire feed on but thy sins?

The more thou sparest thyself now, and followest the flesh, the more grievously shalt thou suffer hereafter, and the more fuel dost thou lay up for that fire.

In what things a man has more sinned, in those shall he be more heavily punished.

There the slothful shall be pricked forward with burning goads, and the glutton will be tormented with extreme hunger and thirst.

There the luxurious and the lovers of pleasure will be covered all over with burning pitch and stinking brimstone, and the envious, like mad dogs, will howl for grief.

4. There is no vice which will not have its proper torments.

There the proud will be filled with all confusion; and the covetous be straitened with most miserable want.

There one hour of suffering will be more sharp, than a hundred years here spent in the most rigid penance.

There is no rest, no comfort for the damned: but here there is sometimes intermission of labour, and we receive comfort from our friends.

Be careful at present, and sorrowful for thy sins: that in the day of judgment thou mayest be secure with the blessed.

For then the just shall stand with great constancy against those that afflicted and oppressed them. Wisdom v.

Then will he stand to judge: who now humbly submits himself to the judgment of men.

Then the poor and humble will have great confidence: and the proud will fear on every side.

5. Then it will appear that he was wise in this world, who learned for Christ's sake to be a fool, and despised.

Then all tribulation suffered with patience will be pleasing, *and all iniquity shall stop her mouth*. Psalms cvi.

Then every devout person will rejoice, and the irreligious will be sad.

Then the flesh that has been mortified shall triumph more than if it had always been pampered in delights.

Then shall the mean habit shine, and fine clothing appear contemptible.

Then shall the poor cottage be more commended than the gilded palace.

Then constant patience shall more avail, than all the power of the world.

Then simple obedience shall be more prized, than all worldly craftiness.

6. Then a pure and good conscience shall be a greater subject of joy, than learned philosophy.

Then the contempt of riches shall weigh more than all the treasures of worldlings.

Then wilt thou be more comforted that thou hast prayed devoutly, than that thou hast fared daintily.

Then wilt thou rejoice more that thou hast kept silence, than that thou hast made long discourses, or talked much.

Then will holy works be of greater value than many fair words.

Then will a strict life and hard penance be more pleasing than all the delights of the earth.

Learn at present to suffer in little things, that then thou mayest be delivered from more grievous sufferings.

Try first here what thou canst suffer hereafter.

If thou canst now endure so little how wilt thou be able to bear everlasting torments?

If a little suffering now makes thee so impatient, what will hell fire do hereafter?

Surely thou canst not have thy pleasure in this world, and afterwards reign with Christ.

7. If to this day thou hadst always lived in honours and pleasures: what would it avail thee, if thou wert now in a moment to die?

All then is vanity, but to love God, and to serve him alone!

For he that loves God with his whole heart, neither fears death, nor punishment, nor judgment, nor hell: because perfect love gives secure access to God.

But he that is yet delighted with sin, no wonder if he be afraid of death and judgment.

It is good, however, that if love, as yet, reclaim thee not from evil, at least the fear of hell restrain thee.

But he that lays aside the fear of God, will not be able to continue long in good, but will quickly fall into the snares of the devil.

CHAPTER XXV.
OF THE FERVENT AMENDMENT OF OUR WHOLE LIFE.

1. Be vigilant, and delight in God's service, and often think with thyself, to what end thou camest hither, and why thou didst leave the world: was it not that thou mightest live to God, and become a spiritual man?

Be fervent therefore in thy spiritual progress, for thou shalt shortly receive the reward of thy labours: and then grief and fear shall no more come near thee.

Thou shalt labour now a little, and thou shalt find great rest: yea, everlasting joy.

If thou continue faithful and fervent in working, God will doubtless be faithful and liberal in rewarding.

Thou must preserve a good and firm hope of coming to the crown: but must not think thyself secure, lest thou grow negligent or proud.

2. When a certain person in anxiety of mind was often wavering between hope and fear; and on a time being overwhelmed with grief, had prostrated himself in prayer in the church before a certain altar, he revolved these things within himself, saying: *If I did but know that I should still persevere*: and presently he heard within himself an answer from God: *And if thou didst know this, what wouldst thou do? Do now what thou wouldst then do, and thou shalt be very secure*.

And immediately being comforted and strengthened, he committed himself to the divine will, and his anxious wavering ceased.

Neither had he a mind any more to search curiously, to know what should befal him hereafter; but rather studied to enquire what was the will of God, *well pleasing and perfect*, for the beginning and accomplishing every good work.

Hope in the Lord, and do good, saith the prophet, and inhabit the land, and thou shalt be fed with the riches thereof. Psalms xxxi.

There is one thing which keeps many back from spiritual progress and fervent amendment of life, and that is, the apprehension of difficulty, or the labour which must be gone through in the conflict.

And they indeed advance most of all others in virtue, who strive manfully to overcome those things which they find more troublesome or contrary to them.

For there a man makes greater progress, and merits greater grace, where he overcomes himself more, and mortifies himself in spirit.

4. But all men have not alike to overcome and mortify.

Yet he that is diligent and zealous, although he have more passions to fight against, will be able to make a greater progress than another who has fewer passions, but is withal less fervent in the pursuit of virtues.

Two things particularly conduce to a great amendment: these are forcibly to withdraw one's self from that to which nature is viciously inclined, and earnestly to labour for that good which one wants the most.

Study likewise to fly more carefully, and to overcome those faults which most frequently displease thee in others.

5. Turn all occasions to thy spiritual profit: so that if thou seest or hearest any good examples, thou mayest be spurred on to imitate them.

But if thou observe any thing that is blame-worthy, take heed thou commit not the same: or if thou at any time hast done it, labour to amend it out of hand.

As thine eye observeth others: so art thou also observed by others.

O how sweet and comfortable it is to see brethren fervent and devout, regular and well disciplined!

How sad a thing, and how afflicting, to see such walk disorderly, and who practise nothing of what they are called to.

How hurtful it is to neglect the intent of our vocation, and to turn our minds to things that are not our business.

6. Be mindful of the resolution thou hast taken, and set before thee the image of the *crucifix*.

Well mayest thou be ashamed, if thou looked upon the life of Jesus Christ, that thou hast not yet studied to conform thyself more to his pattern, although thou hast been long in the way of God.

A religious man, who exercises himself seriously and devoutly in the most holy life and passion of our Lord, shall find there abundantly all things profitable and necessary for him: nor need he seek for any thing better out of Jesus.

O if our crucified Jesus did but come into our heart, how quickly and sufficiently learned should we be!

7. A fervent religious man bears and takes all things well that are commanded him.

A negligent and lukewarm religious man has trouble upon trouble, and on every side suffers anguish: because he has no comfort within, and is hindered from seeking any without.

A religious man that lives not in discipline, lies open to dreadful ruin.

He that seeks to be more loose and remiss will always be uneasy: for one thing or other will always displease him.

8. How do so many other religious do, who live under strict monastic discipline?

They seldom go abroad; they live very retired; their diet is very poor; their habit coarse; they labour much; they speak little; they watch long; they rise early; they spend much time in prayer; they read often; and keep themselves in all kind of discipline.

Consider the *Carthusians*, the *Cistercians*, and the monks and nuns of divers orders: how every night they rise to sing psalms to the Lord.

It would therefore be a shame for thee to be sluggish at so holy a time, when such multitudes of religious begin with joy to give praises to God.

9. O that we had nothing else to do but to praise the Lord our God with our whole heart and mouth!

O that thou didst never want to eat, nor drink, nor sleep, but couldst always praise God, and be employed solely in spiritual exercises!

Thou wouldst then be much more happy than now, whilst thou art under the necessity of serving the flesh.

Would to God there were no such necessities, but only the spiritual refreshments of the soul, which, alas, we taste too seldom!

10. When a man is come to this, that he seeks his comfort from nothing created, then he begins perfectly to relish God; then likewise will he be well content, however matters happen to him.

Then will he neither rejoice for much, nor be sorrowful for little: but will commit himself wholly and confidently to God, who is to him all in all; to whom nothing perishes or dies, but all things live to him, and serve him at a beck without delay.

11. Always remember thy end, and that time once lost never returns.

Without care and diligence thou shalt never acquire virtues.

If thou beginnest to grow lukewarm, thou wilt begin to be uneasy.

But if thou givest thyself to fervour, thou shalt find great peace: and the grace of God, and love of virtue will make thee feel less labour.

A fervent and diligent man is ready for all things.

It is a greater labour to resist vices and passions, than to toil at bodily labours.

He that does not shun small defects, by little and little falls into greater.

Thou wilt always rejoice in the evening, if thou spend the day profitably.

Watch over thyself, stir up thyself, admonish thyself; and whatever becometh of others, neglect not thyself.

The greater violence thou offerest to thyself, the greater progress thou wilt make. **Amen**.

End Of Book I.

THE IMITATION OF CHRIST.

BOOK II.

CHAPTER I.
OF INTERIOR CONVERSATION.

1. The kingdom of God is within you, saith the Lord. Luke vii.

Convert thyself with thy whole heart to the Lord: and quit this miserable world, and thy soul shall find rest.

Learn to despise exterior things, and give thyself to the interior, and thou shalt see the kingdom of God will come into thee.

For the kingdom of God is peace and joy in the Holy Ghost, which is not given to the wicked.

Christ will come to thee, discovering to thee his consolation, if thou wilt prepare him a fit dwelling within thee.

All his glory and beauty is in the interior, and there he pleaseth himself.

Many a visit doth he make to the ***internal man***, sweet is his communication with him, delightful his consolation, much peace, and a familiarity exceedingly to be admired.

2. O faithful soul, prepare thy heart for this thy Spouse, that he may vouchsafe to come to thee, and dwell in thee.

For so he saith: If any man love me, he will keep my word, and we will come to him, and we will make our abode with him. John xiv.

Make room then for Christ within thee, and deny entrance to all others.

When thou hast Christ, thou art rich, and he is sufficient for thee: he will provide for thee, and will be thy faithful ***Procurator*** in all things, so that thou needest not trust to men.

For men quickly change, and presently fail: but Christ remainis forever, and stands by us firmly to the end.

3. There is no great confidence to be put in a frail mortal man, though he be profitable and beloved: nor much grief to be taken, if sometimes he be against thee and cross thee.

They that are with thee to-day, maybe against thee to-morrow: and on the other hand often change like the wind.

Place thy whole confidence in God, and let him be thy fear and thy love; he will answer for thee, and do for thee what is for the best.

Thou hast not here a lasting city: and wherever thou art, thou art a stranger and a pilgrim: nor wilt thou ever have rest, unless thou be interiorly united to Christ.

4. Why dost thou stand looking about thee here, since this is not thy resting place?

Thy dwelling must be in heaven: and all things of the earth are only to be looked upon as passing by.

All things pass away, and thou along with them.

See that thou cleave not to them, lest thou be ensnared and lost.

Let thy thought be with the Most High, and thy prayer directed to Christ without intermission.

If thou knowest not how to meditate on high and heavenly things, rest on the passion of Christ, and willingly dwell in his secret wounds.

For if thou fly devoutly to the wounds and precious stigmas of Jesus, thou shalt feel great comfort in tribulation; neither wilt thou much regard the being despised by men, but wilt easily bear up against detracting tongues.

5. Christ was also in this world despised by men: and in his greatest necessity forsaken by his acquaintance and friends in the midst of reproaches.

Christ would suffer and be despised, and dost thou dare to complain of any one?

Christ had adversaries and backbiters, and wouldst thou have all to be thy friends and benefactors?

Whence shall thy patience be crowned, if thou meet with no adversity?

If thou wilt suffer no opposition, how wilt thou be a friend of Christ?

Suffer with Christ and for Christ, if thou desirest to reign with Christ.

6. If thou hadst once perfectly entered into the interior of Jesus, and experienced a little of his burning love, then wouldst thou not care at all for thy own convenience or inconvenience, but wouldst rather rejoice at reproach, because the love of Jesus makes a man despise himself.

A love of Jesus and of *truth*, and a true internal man, that is free from inordinate affections, can freely turn himself to God, and in spirit elevate himself above himself, and rest in enjoyment.

7. He to whom all things relish as they are, *viz.* in God, who is the very truth, not as they are said or esteemed to be, he is wise indeed, and taught rather by God than men.

He who knows how to walk internally, and to make little account of external things, is not at a loss for proper places or times for performing devout exercises.

An internal man quickly recollects himself, because he never pours forth his whole self upon outward things.

Exterior labour is no prejudice to him, nor any employment which for a time is necessary; but as things fall out, he so accommodates himself to them.

He that is well disposed and orderly in his interior, heeds not the strange and perverse carriages of men.

As much as a man draws things to himself, so much is he hindered and distracted by them.

8. If thou hadst a right spirit within thee, and wert purified from earthly affections, all things would turn to thy good and to thy profit.

For this reason do many things displease thee, and often trouble thee; because thou art not as yet perfectly dead to thyself, nor separated from all earthly things.

Nothing so defiles and entangles the heart of man, as impure love to created things.

If thou reject exterior comfort, thou wilt be able to contemplate heavenly things, and frequently to feel excessive joy interiorly.

CHAPTER II.
OF HUMBLE SUBMISSION.

1. Make no great account who is for thee, or against thee; but let it be thy business and thy care, that God may be with thee in every thing thou dost.

Have a good conscience, and God will sufficiently defend thee.

For he whom God will help, no man's malice can hurt.

If thou canst but hold thy peace and suffer, thou shalt see without doubt that the Lord will help thee.

He knows the time and manner of delivering thee, and therefore thou must resign thyself to him.

It belongs to God to help and to deliver us from all confusion.

Oftentimes it is very profitable for the keeping us in greater humility, that others know and reprehend our faults.

2. When a man humbles himself for his defects, he then easily appeases others, and quickly satisfies those that are angry with him.

The humble man, God protects and delivers: the humble he loves and comforts: to the humble he inclines himself: to the humble he gives grace: and after he has been depressed, raises him to glory.

To the humble he reveals his secrets, and sweetly draws and invites him to himself.

The humble man having received reproach, maintains himself well enough in peace: because he is fixed in God, and not in the world.

Never think thou hast made any progress, till thou look upon thyself inferior to all.

CHAPTER III.
OF A GOOD PEACEABLE MAN.

1. Keep thyself first in peace, and then thou wilt be able to bring others to peace.

A peaceable man does more good, than one that is very learned.

A passionate man turns every good into evil, and easily believes evil.

A good peaceable man turns all things to good.

He that is in perfect peace, suspects no man: but he that is discontented and disturbed, is tossed about with various suspicions: he is neither easy himself, nor does he suffer others to be easy.

He often says that which he should not say: and omit that which would be better for him to do.

He considers what others are obliged to do: and neglects that to which he himself is obliged.

Have therefore a zeal in the first place over thyself, and then thou mayest justly exercise thy zeal towards thy neighbour.

2. Thou knowest well enough how to excuse and colour thy own doings, and thou wilt not take the excuses of others.

It were more just that thou shouldst accuse thyself, and excuse thy brother.

If thou wilt be borne withal, bear also with another.

See how far thou art yet from true charity and humility, which knows not how to be angry with any one, or to have indignation against any one but one's self.

It is no great thing to be able to converse with them that are good and meek: for this is naturally pleasing to all.

And every one would willingly have peace, and love those best that agree with them.

But to live peaceably with those that are harsh and perverse, or disorderly, or such as oppose us, is a great grace, and a highly commendable and manly exploit.

3. Some there are that keep themselves in peace, and have peace also with others.

And there are some that are neither at peace within themselves, nor suffer others to be in peace: they are troublesome to others, but always more troublesome to themselves.

And some there are who keep themselves in peace, and study to restore peace to others.

Yet all our peace in this miserable life is rather to be placed in humble suffering, than in not feeling adversities.

He who knows how to suffer, will enjoy much peace.

Such a one is conqueror of himself, and Lord of the world, a friend of Christ and heir of heaven.

CHAPTER IV.
OF A PURE MIND AND SIMPLE INTENTION.

1. With two wings a man is lifted up above earthly things; that is, with *simplicity* and *purity*.

Simplicity must be in the intention, *purity* in the affection.

Simplicity aims at God, *purity* takes hold of him, and tastes him.

No good action will hinder thee, if thou be free from inordinate affection.

If thou intendest and seekest nothing else but the will of God, and the profit of thy neighbour, thou shalt enjoy internal liberty.

If thy heart were right, then every creature would be to thee a looking-glass of life, and a book of holy doctrine.

There is no creature so little and contemptible as not to manifest the goodness of God.

2. If thou wert good and pure within, then wouldst thou discern all things without impediment, and understand them right.

A pure heart penetrates heaven and hell.

According as every one is interiorly, so he judgeth exteriorly.

If there be joy in the world, certainly the man whose heart is pure enjoys it.

And if there be any where tribulation and anguish, an evil conscience feels the most of it.

As iron put into the fire loses the rust, and becomes all fire; so a man that turns himself wholly to God puts off his sluggishness, and is changed into a new man.

4. When a man begins to grow lukewarm, he is afraid of a little labour, and willingly takes external comfort.

But when he begins perfectly to overcome himself, and to walk manfully in the way of God, then he makes less account of those things, which before he considered burthensome to him.

CHAPTER V.
OF THE CONSIDERATION OF ONE'S SELF.

1. We cannot trust much to ourselves, because we often want grace and understanding.

There is but little light in us, and this we quickly lose through negligence.

Many times also we perceive not that we are so blind interiorly.

We often do ill, and do worse in excusing it.

We are sometimes moved with passion, and we mistake it for zeal.

We blame little things in others, and pass over great things in ourselves.

We are quick enough at perceiving and weighing what we suffer from others: but we mind not what others suffer from us.

He that would well and duly weigh his own deeds, would have no room to judge hard of others.

2. An internal man prefers the care of himself before all other cares: and he that diligently attends to himself is easily silent with regard to others.

Thou wilt never be internal and devout, unless thou pass over in silence other men's concerns, and particularly look to thyself.

If thou attend wholly to thyself, and to God, thou wilt be little moved with what thou perceivest without thee.

Where art thou, when thou art not present to thyself?

And when thou hast run over all things, what profit will it be to thee, if thou hast neglected thyself?

If thou desirest to have peace and true union, thou must set all the rest aside, and turn thy eyes upon thyself alone.

3. Thou wilt then make great progress, if thou keep thyself free from all temporal care.

But if thou set a value upon any thing temporal, thou wilt fail exceedingly.

Let nothing be great in thy eyes, nothing high, nothing pleasant, nothing agreeable to thee, except it be purely God, or of God.

Look upon as vain, all the comfort which thou meetest with from any creature.

A soul that loveth God despiseth all things that are less than God.

None but God eternal and incomprehensible, who fills all things, is the comfort of the soul, and the true joy of the heart.

CHAPTER VI.
OF THE JOY OF A GOOD CONSCIENCE.

1. The glory of a good man, is the testimony of a good conscience. Keep a good conscience, and thou shall always have joy.

A good conscience can bear very much, and is very joyful in the midst of adversity.

A bad conscience is always fearful and uneasy.

Sweetly wilt thou take thy rest, if thy heart reprehend thee not.

Never rejoice but when thou hast done well.

The wicked never have true joy, neither do they feel internal peace; because, *There is no peace to the wicked*, saith the Lord. *Isaiah* xlviii.

And if they shall say, we are in peace, evils will not come upon us, and who shall dare to hurt us, believe them not; for the wrath of God shall rise on a sudden, and their deeds will be brought to nothing, and their projects shall perish.

2. To glory in tribulation is not hard to him that loves: for so to glory is to glory in the cross of our Lord.

That glory is short lived, which is given and taken by men.

The glory of this world is always accompanied with sorrow.

The glory of good men is in their own consciences, not in the mouths of others.

The joy of the just is from God, and in God: and they rejoice in the *truth*.

He that desires true and everlasting glory, values not that which is temporal.

And he that seeks after temporal glory, or does not heartily despise it, shews himself to have little love for that which is heavenly.

That man has great tranquillity of heart, who neither cares for praises nor dispraises.

3. He will easily be content, and in peace, whose conscience is clean.

Thou art not more holy, if thou art praised: nor any thing the worse, if thou art dispraised.

What thou art, that thou art: nor canst thou be said to be greater than God sees thee to be.

If thou considerest well what thou art within thyself, thou wilt not care what men say of thee.

Man beholds the face; but God looks upon the heart.

Man considers the actions; but God weighs the intentions.

To do always well, and to hold one's self in small account, is a mark of an humble soul.

To refuse a comfort from any created thing, is a sign of great purity and interior confidence.

4. He that seeks no outward testimony for himself, shews plainly, that he has committed himself wholly to God.

For not he that commendeth himself, saith St. Paul, is approved, but he whom God commendeth. 2 Corinthians x.

To walk with God *within*, and not to be held by any affection *without*, is the state of an *internal* man.

CHAPTER VII.
OF THE LOVE OF JESUS ABOVE ALL THINGS.

1. Blessed is he who knows what it is to love Jesus, and to despise himself for the sake of Jesus.

We must quit what we love for *this* Beloved, because Jesus will be loved alone above all things.

The love of things created is deceitful and inconstant: the love of Jesus is faithful and perseverant.

He that cleaveth to creatures shall fall with them.

He that embraceth Jesus shall stand firm for ever.

Love him, and keep him for thy friend; who, when all go away, will not leave thee, nor suffer thee to perish in the end.

Thou must at last be separated from all things else, whether thou wilt or not.

2. Keep thyself with Jesus both in life and death, and commit thyself to his trust who alone can help thee, when all others fail.

Thy beloved is of such a nature, that he will admit of no other: but will have thy heart to himself, and sit there like a king on his own throne.

If thou couldst but purge thyself well from affection to creatures, Jesus would willingly dwell with thee.

Thou wilt find all that in a manner loss, which thou hast placed in men out of Jesus.

Do not trust nor rely upon a windy reed: For all flesh is grass, and all the glory thereof shall fade like the flower of the grass. Isaiah xl.

3. Thou wilt soon be deceived, if thou only regard the outward shew of men.

For if thou seek thy comfort and thy gain in others, thou wilt often meet with loss.

If in all thou seek Jesus, doubtless thou wilt find Jesus.

But if thou seek thyself, thou wilt indeed find thyself, but to thy own ruin.

For a man does himself more harm if he seek not Jesus, than the whole world and all his enemies could do him.

CHAPTER VIII.
OF FAMILIAR FRIENDSHIP WITH JESUS.

1. When Jesus is present, all goes well, and nothing seems difficult: but when Jesus is absent every thing is hard.

When Jesus speaks not within, our comfort is worth nothing: but if Jesus speak but one word, we feel a great consolation.

Did not Mary Magdalen arise presently from the place where she wept, when Martha said to her: *The Master is here and calls for thee*. John xiii.

Happy hour, when Jesus calls from tears, to joy of spirit!

How dry and hard art thou without Jesus! How foolish and vain if thou desire any thing out of Jesus! Is not this a greater damage than if thou wert to lose the whole world?

2. What can the world profit thee without Jesus?

To be without Jesus is a grievous hell, and to be with Jesus a sweet paradise.

If Jesus be with thee, no enemy can hurt thee.

Whoever finds Jesus, finds a good treasure, yea good above all goods.

And he that loseth Jesus, loseth exceeding much, and more than if he lost the whole world.

He is wretchedly poor, who lives without Jesus: and he is exceedingly rich, who is well with Jesus.

3. It is a great art to know how to converse with Jesus: and to know how to keep Jesus is great wisdom.

Be humble and peaceable, and Jesus will be with thee.

Be devout and quiet, and Jesus will stay with thee.

Thou mayest quickly drive away Jesus and lose his grace, if thou decline after outward things.

And if thou drive him from thee, and lose him, to whom wilt thou fly, and whom then wilt thou seek for thy friend?

Without a friend thou canst not well live; and if Jesus be not thy friend above all, thou wilt be exceeding sad and desolate.

Thou actest then foolishly, if thou puttest thy trust or rejoiceth in any other.

We ought rather to chuse to have the whole world against us, than to offend Jesus.

Of all therefore that are dear to thee, let Jesus always be thy special beloved.

4. Let all be loved for Jesus's sake, but Jesus for himself.

Jesus Christ alone is singularly to be loved, who alone is found good and faithful above all friends.

For him, and in him, let both friends and enemies be dear to thee: and for all these must thou pray to him, that all may know and love him.

Neither desire to be singularly praised or beloved: for this belongs to God alone, who hath none like to himself.

Neither desire that any one's heart should be set on thee: nor do thou let thyself be taken up with the love of any one: but let Jesus be in thee, and in every good man.

5. Be pure and free interiorly, without being entangled by any creature.

Thou must be naked and carry a pure heart to God, if thou wilt attend at leisure, and see how sweet is the Lord.

And indeed thou wilt never attain to this, unless thou be prevented and drawn in by his grace: that so thou mayest all *alone* be united to him *alone*, having cast out and dismissed all others.

For when the grace of God comes to a man, then he is strong and powerful for all things: and when it departs, then he is poor and weak, left as it were only to stripes.

In these he must not be dejected nor despair; but stand with an even mind, resigned to the will of God, and bear, for the glory of Jesus Christ, whatever shall befal him: because after winter, comes summer; after night the day returns; after a storm there follows a great calm.

CHAPTER IX.
OF THE WANT OF ALL COMFORT.

1. It is not hard to despise all human comfort, when we have divine.

But it is much, and very much, to be able to want all comfort, both human and divine: and to be willing to bear this interior banishment for God's honour, and to seek one's self in nothing, nor to think of one's own merit.

What great thing is it, if thou be cheerful and devout when grace comes? This hour is desirable to all.

He rides at ease, that is carried by the grace of God.

And what wonder, if he feels no weight, who is carried by the Almighty, and led on by the sovereign guide?

2. We willingly would have something to comfort us: and it is with difficulty that a man can put off himself.

The holy martyr, Lawrence, overcame the world, with his prelate; because he despised whatever seemed delightful in this world; and for the love of Christ he also suffered the High Priest of God, *Sixtus*, whom he exceedingly loved, to be taken away from him.

He overcame therefore the love of man by the love of the Creator: and instead of the comfort he had in man, he made choice rather of God's pleasure.

So do thou also learn to part with a necessary and beloved friend for the love of God.

And take it not to heart when thou art forsaken by a friend: knowing that one time or other we must all part.

3. A man must go through a long and great conflict in himself, before he can learn fully to overcome himself, and to draw his whole affection towards God.

When a man stands upon himself, he easily declines after human comforts.

But a true lover of Christ, and a diligent pursuer of virtues, does not hunt after comforts, nor seek such sensible sweetnesses: but is rather willing to bear strong trials and hard labours for Christ.

4. Therefore when God gives spiritual comfort, receive it with thanksgiving; but know that it is the bounty of God, not thy merit.

Be not puffed up, be not overjoyed, nor vainly presume: but rather be the more humble for this gift, and the more cautious and fearful in all thy actions: for this hour will pass away, and temptation will follow.

When comfort shall be taken away from thee, do not presently despair; but wait with humility and patience for the heavenly visit: for God is able to restore thee a greater consolation.

This is no new thing, nor strange to those who have experienced the ways of God: for in the great saints and ancient prophets there has often been this kind of variety.

5. Hence one said: at the time when grace was with him: *I said in my abundance, I shall not be moved for ever*. Psalms xxix.

But when grace was retired, he immediately tells us what he experienced in himself: *Thou hast turned away thy face from me, and I became troubled*.

Yet, in the mean time he despairs not, but more earnestly prays to our Lord, and says: *To thee, O Lord, will I cry, and I will pray to my God*.

Lastly, he receives the fruit of his prayer: and witnesses that he was heard, saying: *The Lord hath heard me, and hath had mercy on me: The Lord is become my helper*.

But in what manner? Thou hast turned, says he, my mourning into joy to me, and thou hast encompassed me with gladness.

If it has been thus with great saints, we that are weak and poor must not be discouraged, if we are sometimes in fervour, sometimes cold: because the Spirit comes and goes according to his own good pleasure.

Wherefore holy Job says: Thou dost visit him early in the morning, and on a sudden thou triest him. Job vii.

6. Wherein then can I hope, or in what must I put my trust, but in God's great mercy alone, and in the hope of heavenly grace!

For whether I have with me good men, or devout brethren, or faithful friends, or holy books, or fine treatises, or sweet singing and hymns: all these help little, and give me but little relish, when I am forsaken by grace, and left in my own poverty.

At such a time there is no better remedy than patience, and leaving myself to God's will.

7. I never found any one so religious and devout, as not to have sometimes a subtraction of grace, or feel a diminution of fervour.

No saint was ever so highly wrapt and illuminated, as not to be tempted at first or at last.

For he is not worthy of the high contemplation of God, who has not, for God's sake, been exercised with some tribulation.

For temptation going before, is usually a sign of ensuing consolation.

For heavenly comfort is promised to such has have been proved by temptations.

To him that shall overcome, saith our Lord, *I will give to eat of the tree of life*. Apoc. ii.

[USCCB: Revelation ii. 7]

8. Now divine consolation is given that a man may be better able to support adversities.

And temptation follows, that he may not be proud of good.

The devil never sleeps, neither is the flesh yet dead: therefore thou must not cease to prepare thyself for battle, for on the right hand, and on the left, are enemies that never rest.

CHAPTER X.
OF GRATITUDE FOR THE GRACE OF GOD.

1. Why seekest thou rest, since thou art born to labour?

Dispose thyself to patience, rather than consolation: and to bear the cross, rather than to rejoice.

For who is there amongst worldly people, that would not willingly receive comfort and spiritual joy, if he could always have it?

For spiritual consolations exceed all the delight of the world, and pleasures of the flesh.

For all worldly delights are either vain or filthy: but spiritual delights alone are pleasant and honest, springing from virtue, and infused by God into pure minds.

But these divine consolations no man can always enjoy when he will: because the time of temptation is not long away.

2. But what very much opposes these heavenly visits, is a false liberty of mind, and a great confidence in one's self.

God does well in giving the grace of consolation: but man does ill in not returning it all to God with thanksgiving.

And this is the reason why the gifts of grace cannot flow in us: because we are ungrateful to the Giver: nor do we return all to the fountain's head.

For grace is ever due to him that duly returns thanks: and what is wont to be given to the humble, will be taken away from the proud.

3. I would not have any such consolation as should rob me of compunction: nor do I wish to have such contemplation as leads to pride.

For all that is high, is not holy; nor all that is pleasant, good: nor every desire, pure; nor is every thing that is dear to us, pleasing to God.

I willingly accept of that grace, which makes me always more humble and fearful, and more ready to forsake myself.

He that has been taught by the gift of grace, and instructed by the scourge of the withdrawing of it, will not dare to attribute any thing of good to himself; but will rather confess himself to be poor and naked.

Give to God what is his, and take to thyself what is thine: that is, give thanks to God for his grace; but as to thyself be sensible that nothing is to be attributed to thee, but sin, and the punishment due to sin.

4. Put thyself always in the lowest place, and the highest shall be given thee: for the highest stands not without the lowest.

The saints that are highest in the sight of God, are the least in their own eyes: and the more glorious they are, the more humble they are in themselves.

Being full of the truth and heavenly glory, they are not desirous of vain glory.

They that are grounded and established in God, can by no means be proud.

And they that attribute to God all whatsoever good they have received, seek not glory from one another, but that glory which is from God alone: and desire above all things that God may be praised in themselves, and in all the saints, and to this same they always tend.

5. Be grateful then for the least, and thou shalt be worthy to receive greater things.

Let the least be to thee as something very great, and the most contemptible as a special favour.

If thou considerest the dignity of the Giver, no gift will seem to thee little which is given by so great a God.

Yea, though he gives punishment and stripes, it ought to be acceptable: for whatever he suffers to befal us, he always does it for our salvation.

He that desires to retain the grace of God, let him be thankful for grace when it is given, and patient when it is withdrawn.

Let him pray, that it may return: let him be cautious and humble, lest he lose it.

CHAPTER XI.
OF THE SMALL NUMBER OF THE LOVERS OF THE CROSS OF JESUS.

1. Jesus has now many lovers of his heavenly kingdom: but few that are willing to bear the cross.

He has many that are desirous of comfort, but few of tribulation.

He finds many companions of his table, but few of his abstinence.

All desire to rejoice with him: few are willing to suffer for him.

Many follow Jesus to the breaking of bread; but few to the drinking the chalice of his passion.

Many reverence his miracles; but few follow the ignominy of his cross.

Many love Jesus as long as they meet with no adversity; many praise him and bless him as long as they receive consolations from him.

But if Jesus hide himself and leave them for a little while; they either fall into complaints, or excessive dejection.

2. But they that love Jesus for Jesus's sake, and not for any comfort of their own, bless him no less in tribulation and anguish of heart, than in the greatest consolation.

And if he should never give them his comfort, yet would they always praise him, and always give him thanks.

3. O! how much is the pure love of Jesus able to do, when it is not mixed with any self-interest or self-love!

Are not all those to be called hirelings, who are always seeking consolations!

Are they not convinced to be rather lovers of themselves than of Christ, who are always thinking of their own profit and gain?

Where shall we find a man that is willing to serve God *gratis?*

4. Seldom do we find any one so spiritual, as to be stripped of all things.

For who shall be able to find the man that is truly poor in spirit, and naked of all things created? His value is (as of things that is brought) *from afar and from the remotest coasts*, Proverbs xxxi.

If a man gives his whole substance, it is yet nothing.

And if he do great penance, it is yet little.

And if he attain to all knowledge, he is far off still.

And if he have great virtue, and exceeding fervent devotion, there is still much wanting to him; to wit, one thing, which is chiefly necessary for him.

And what is that? That having left all things else, he leave also himself and wholly get out of himself, and retain nothing of self-love.

And when he shall have done all things which he knows should be done, let him think that he has done nothing.

5. Let him not make great account of that which may appear much to be esteemed: but let him in *truth* acknowledge himself to be an unprofitable servant: as truth itself has said, *When ye shall have done all that is commanded you, say, We are unprofitable servants.* Luke xvii.

Then may he be truly poor and naked in spirit, and may say with the prophet, *I am all alone, and poor*. Psalms xxiv.

THOMAS À KEMPIS

[USCCB: Psalms xxv, 16.]

Yet no one is indeed richer than such a man, none more powerful, none more free; who knows how to leave himself and all things, and place himself in the very lowest place.

CHAPTER XII.
OF THE KING'S HIGHWAY OF THE HOLY CROSS.

1. To many this seems a hard saying: *Deny thyself, take up thy cross and follow Jesus*. Matthew xvi.

But it will be much harder to hear that last word: *Depart from me you cursed into everlasting fire*. Matthew xxv.

For they that at present willingly hear and follow the word of the cross, shall not then be afraid of eternal condemnation.

The sign of the cross will be in heaven, when the Lord shall come to judge.

Then all the servants of the cross, who in their life time have conformed themselves to him that was crucified, shall come to Christ their judge with great confidence.

2. Why then art thou afraid to take up thy cross, which leads to a kingdom?

In the cross is salvation: in the cross is life: in the cross is protection from thy enemies.

In the cross is infusion of heavenly sweetness: in the cross is strength of mind: in the cross is joy of spirit.

In the cross is the height of virtue: in the cross is the perfection of sanctity.

There is no health of the soul, nor hope of eternal life, but in the cross.

Take up therefore thy cross and follow Jesus, and thou shalt go into life everlasting.

He is gone before thee, carrying his cross: and he died for thee upon the cross: that thou mayest also bear thy cross, and love to die on the cross.

Because, if thou die with him, thou shalt also live with him; and if thou art his companion in buffering, thou shalt also partake in his glory.

3. Behold the cross is all, and in dying [to thyself] all consists: and there is no other way to life, and to true internal peace, but the way of the holy cross, and of daily mortification.

Go where thou wilt, seek what thou wilt, and thou shalt not find a higher way above, nor a safer way below, than the way of the holy cross.

Dispose and order all things according as thou wilt; and as seems best to thee; and thou shalt still find something to suffer, either willingly or unwillingly, and so thou shalt still find the cross.

For either thou shalt feel pain in the body, or sustain in thy soul tribulation of spirit.

4. Sometimes thou shalt be left by God, other times thou shalt be afflicted by thy neighbour: and what is more, thou shalt often be a trouble to thyself.

Neither canst thou be delivered or eased by any remedy or comfort, but as long as it shall please God, thou must bear it.

For God would have thee learn to suffer tribulation without comfort, and wholly to submit thyself to him, and to become more humble by tribulation.

No man hath so lively a feeling of the passion of Christ, as he who hath happened to suffer such like things.

The cross therefore is always ready, and every where waits for thee.

Thou canst not escape it, whithersoever thou runnest: for whithersoever thou goest, thou carriest thyself with thee, and shall always find thyself.

Turn thyself upwards, or turn thyself downwards: turn thyself without, or turn thyself within thee: and every where thou shalt find the cross.

And every where thou must of necessity have patience if thou desirest inward peace, and wouldst merit an eternal crown.

5. If thou carry the cross willingly, it will carry thee, and bring thee to thy desired end; to wit, to that place where there will be an end of suffering, tho' here there will be none.

If thou carry it unwillingly, thou makest it a burden to thee, and loadest thyself the more: and nevertheless thou must bear it.

If thou fling away one cross, without doubt thou wilt find another, and perhaps a heavier.

6. Dost thou think to escape that which no mortal could ever avoid? What saint was there ever in the world without his cross and affliction?

Our Lord Jesus Christ himself was not one hour of his life without suffering: *It behoved*, saith he, *that Christ should suffer, and rise from the dead, and so enter into his glory*. Luke xxiv.

And how dost thou pretend to seek another way than the royal way, which is the way of the holy cross.

7. The whole life of Christ was a cross, and a martyrdom: and dost thou seek rest and joy?

Thou errest, thou errest, if thou seekest any other thing than to suffer tribulations: for this whole mortal life is full of miseries, and beset on all sides with crosses.

And the higher a person is advanced in spirit, the heavier crosses shall he often meet with: because the pain of his banishment increases in proportion to his love.

8. Yet this man, thus many ways afflicted, is not without some allay of comfort for his ease: because he is sensible of the great profit which he reaps by bearing the cross.

For whilst he willingly resigns himself to it, all the burden of tribulation is converted into an assured hope of comfort from God.

And the more the flesh is brought down by affliction, the more the spirit is strengthened by inward grace.

And sometimes gains such force through affection to tribulation and adversity, by reason of loving to be conformable to the cross of Christ, as not to be willing to be without suffering and affliction: because such a one believes himself by so much the more acceptable to God, as he shall be able to bear more and greater things for him.

This is not man's power, but the grace of Christ, which can and does effect such great things in frail flesh, that what it naturally abhors and flies, even this through fervour of spirit it now embraces and loves.

9. It is not according to man's natural inclination to bear the cross, to love the cross, to chastise the body, and bring it under subjection; to fly honours, to be willing to suffer reproaches, to despise one's self, and wish to be despised; to bear all adversities and losses, and to desire no prosperity in this world.

If thou lookest upon thyself, thou canst do nothing of this of thyself.

But if thou confidest in the Lord, strength will be given thee from heaven, and the world and flesh shall be made subject to thee.

Neither shalt thou fear thine enemy the devil, if thou art armed with faith and signed with the cross of Christ.

10. Set thyself then like a good and faithful servant of Christ to bear manfully the cross of thy Lord, crucified for the love of thee.

Prepare thyself to suffer many adversities, and divers evils in this miserable life; for so it will be with thee, wherever thou art: and so indeed wilt thou find it, wheresoever thou hide thyself.

It must be so, and there is no remedy against tribulation and sorrow, but to bear them patiently.

Drink of the Chalice of the Lord lovingly, if thou desirest to be his friend, and to have part with him.

Leave consolations to God, to do with them as best pleaseth him.

But set thou thyself to bear tribulations, and account them the greatest consolations: for the sufferings of this life bear no proportion with the glory to come, although thou alone couldst suffer them all.

11. When thou shalt arrive thus far, that tribulation becomes sweet and savory to thee for the love of Christ: then think that it is well with thee, for thou hast found a paradise upon earth.

As long as suffering seems grievous to thee, and thou seekest to fly from if, so long will it be ill with thee, and the tribulation from which thou fliest will every where follow thee.

12. If thou set thyself to what thou oughtest; that is, to suffer and to die [to thyself], it will quickly be better with thee, and thou shalt find peace.

Although thou shouldst have been wrapped up to the third heaven with St. Paul, thou art not thereby secured that thou shalt suffer no adversity. *I* (said Jesus) **will shew him how great things he must suffer for my name**. Acts ix.

To suffer, therefore, is what waits for thee, if thou wilt love Jesus, and constantly serve him.

13. Would to God thou wert worthy to suffer something for the name of Jesus! how great a glory would be laid up for thee, how great joy would it be to all the saints of God, and how great edification to thy neighbour!

All recommend patience; but, alas! how few are there that desire to suffer!

With good reason oughtest thou willingly to suffer a little for Christ, since many suffer greater things for the world.

14. Know for certain that thou must lead a dying life; and the more a man dies to himself, the more he begins to live to God.

No man is fit to comprehend heavenly things, who has not resigned himself to suffer adversities for Christ.

Nothing is more acceptable to God, nothing more wholesome for thee in this world, than to suffer willingly for Christ.

And if thou wert to chuse, thou oughtest to wish rather to suffer adversities for Christ, than to be delighted with many comforts: because thus wouldst thou be more like to Christ, and more conformable to all the saints.

For our merit and the advancement of our state, consists not in having many gusts and consolations: but rather in bearing great afflictions and tribulations.

15. If, indeed, there had been any thing better, and more beneficial to man's salvation, than suffering, Christ certainly would have shewed it by word and example.

For he manifestly exhorts both his disciples that followed him, and all that desire to follow him, to bear the cross, saying: *If any one will come after me, let him deny himself, and take up his cross, and follow me*. Luke ix. So that when we have read and searched all, let this be the final conclusion, that *through many tribulations we must enter into the kingdom of God*. Acts xix.

[USCCB: Acts xiv. 22.]

End Of Book III.

THE IMITATION OF CHRIST.

BOOK III.

CHAPTER I
OF THE INTERNAL SPEECH OF CHRIST TO A FAITHFUL SOUL.

1. I will hear what the Lord God speaketh in me. Psalms lxxxiv.

[USCCB: Psalms lxxxv. 9.]

Happy is that soul, which heareth the Lord speaking within her: and from his mouth receiveth the word of comfort.

Happy ears, which receive the veins of the divine whisper, and take no notice of the whisperings of the world.

Happy ears indeed, which hearken to truth itself teaching within, and not to the voice which soundeth without.

Happy eyes, which are shut to outward things, and attentive to the interior.

Happy they who penetrate into internal things, and endeavour to prepare themselves more and more by daily exercises to the attaining to heavenly secrets.

Happy they who seek to be wholly intent on God, and who rid themselves of every worldly impediment.

Mind these things, O my soul, and shut the doors of thy sensuality, that thou mayest hear what the Lord thy God speaks within thee.

2. Thus saith thy Beloved: *I am thy salvation*, thy peace, and thy life: keep thyself with me, and thou shalt find peace.

Let alone all transitory things, and seek things eternal.

What are all temporal things, but deceit? and what will all things created avail thee, if thou be forsaken by the Creator?

Cast off then all earthly things, and make thyself agreeable to thy Creator, and faithful to him, that so thou mayest attain to true happiness.

CHAPTER II
THAT TRUTH SPEAKS WITHIN US WITHOUT NOISE OF WORDS.

1. Speak, Lord, for thy servant heareth. 1 Samuel iii.—I am thy servant, give me understanding that I may know thy testimonies. Psalms cxviii.

[USCCB: Psalms cxix. 27.]

Incline my heart to the words of thy mouth: let thy speech distil as the dew.

Heretofore the Children of Israel said to Moses, Speak thou to us, and we will hear: let not the Lord speak to us, lest we die. Exodus xx.

It is not thus, O Lord, it is not thus I pray; but rather with the prophet **Samuel**, I humbly and earnestly entreat thee, **Speak, Lord, for thy servant heareth**.

Let not **Moses**, nor any of the prophets speak to me; but speak thou rather, O Lord God, the inspirer and enlightener of all the prophets; for thou alone without them canst perfectly instruct me; but they without thee will avail me nothing.

2. They may indeed sound forth words, but they give not the spirit.

They speak well; but if thou be silent, they do not set the heart on fire.

They deliver the letter, but thou disclosest the sense.

They publish mysteries, but thou unlockest the meaning of the things signified.

They declare the commandments, but thou enablest to keep them.

They shew the way, but thou givest strength to walk in it.

They work only outwardly, but thou instructest and enlightenest the heart.

They water exteriorly, but thou givest the increase.

They cry out with words, but thou givest understanding to the hearing.

5. Let not then **Moses** speak to me, but thou O Lord my God, the eternal Truth, lest I die and prove fruitless, if I be only outwardly admonished, and not enkindled within.

Lest the word which I have heard and not fulfilled, which I have known and not loved, which I have believed and not observed, rise up in judgment against me.

Speak, then, O Lord, for thy servant heareth; for thou hast the words of eternal life. John vi.

Speak to me, that it may be for some comfort to my soul, and for the amendment of my whole life; and to thy praise and glory, and everlasting honour.

CHAPTER III.
THAT THE WORDS OF GOD ARE TO BE HEARD WITH HUMILITY, AND THAT MANY WEIGH THEM NOT.

1. My Son, hear my words, words most sweet, exceeding all the learning of philosophers, and of the wise men of this world.

My words are *spirit* and *life*, and not to be estimated by the sense of man.

They are not to be drawn to a vain complacence, but are to be heard in silence, and to be received with all humility and great affection.

2. And I said, Blessed is the man, whom thou, O Lord, shalt instruct, and shalt teach him thy law; that thou mayest give him ease from the evil days, (Psalms xciii.); and that he may not be desolate upon earth.

[USCCB: Psalms xciv. 12-13.]

I (saith the Lord) have taught the prophets from the beginning, and even till now I cease not to speak to all; but many are deaf to my voice, and hard.

The greater number listen more willingly to the world, than to God; and follow sooner the desires of the flesh, than the good-will of God.

The world promises things temporal and of small value, and is served with great eagerness: I promise things most excellent and everlasting, and men's hearts are not moved!

Who is there that serves and obeys me in all things, with that great care, with which the world and its lords are served? *Be ashamed, O Sidon*, saith the sea.

And if thou ask why? hear the reason.

For a small living, men run a great way; for eternal life many will scarce once move a foot from the ground.

An inconsiderable gain is sought after; for one penny sometimes men shamefully quarrel; they are not afraid to toil day and night for a trifle, or some slight promise.

4. But, alas! for an unchangeable good, for an inestimable reward, for the highest honour and never-ending glory, they are unwilling to take the least pains.

Be ashamed then, thou slothful servant, that art so apt to complain, seeing that they are more ready to labour for death than thou for life.

They rejoice more in running after *vanity*, than thou in the pursuit of *truth*.

And indeed they are sometimes frustrated of their hopes; but my promise deceives no man, nor sends away empty him that trusts in me.

What I have promised, I will give; what I have said, I will make good; provided a man continue to the end faithful in my love.

I am the rewarder of all the good, and the strong trier of all the devout.

5. Write my words in thy heart, and think diligently on them; for they will be very necessary in the time of temptation.

What thou understandest not when thou readest, thou shalt know in the day of visitation.

I am accustomed to visit my elect [in] two manner of ways, *viz.* by trial and by comfort.

And I read them daily two lessons; one to rebuke their vices, the other to exhort them to the increase of virtues.

He that has my words, and slights them, has that which shall condemn him at the last day.

A Prayer,
To implore the Grace of Devotion.

6. O Lord my God, thou art all my good; and who am I that I should dare to speak to thee.

I am thy most poor servant, and a wretched little worm, much more poor and contemptible than I conceive or dare express.

Yet remember, O Lord, that I am nothing, I have nothing and can do nothing:

Thou alone art good, just and holy; thou canst do all things; thou givest all things; thou fillest all things, leaving only the sinner empty.

Remember thy tender mercies, and fill my heart with thy grace, thou who wilt not have thy works to be empty.

How can I support myself in this wretched life, unless thy mercy and grace strengthen me?

Turn not away thy face from me; delay not thy visitation; withdraw not thy comfort; lest my soul become as earth without water to thee.

O Lord, teach me to do thy will, teach we to converse worthily and humbly in thy sight; for thou art my wisdom, who knowest me in truth, and didst know me before the world was made, and before I was born in the world.

CHAPTER IV.
THAT WE OUGHT TO WALK IN TRUTH AND HUMILITY IN GOD'S PRESENCE.

1. Son, walk before me in *truth*, and always seek me in the simplicity of thy heart.

He that walks before me in *truth* shall be secured from evil occurrences, and *truth* shall deliver him from deceivers, and from the detractions of the wicked.

If *truth* shall deliver thee, thou shalt be *truly* free, and shalt make no account of the *vain* words of men.

Lord, this is true: as thou sayest, so I beseech thee, let it be done with me. Let thy *truth* teach me, let thy *truth* guard me, and keep me till I come to a happy end.

Let the same deliver me from all evil affections, and all inordinate love, and I shall walk with thee in great liberty of heart.

2. I will teach thee (saith *Truth*) those things that are right and pleasing in my sight.

Think on thy sins with great compunction and sorrow; and never esteem thyself to be any thing for thy good works.

Thou art indeed a sinner, subject to and intangled with many passions.

Of thyself thou always tendest to nothing, thou quickly fallest, thou art quickly overcome, easily disturbed and dissolved.

Thou hast not any thing in which thou canst glory, but many things for which thou oughtest to vilify thyself; for thou art much weaker than thou art able to comprehend.

3. Let nothing then seem much to thee of all thou doest:

Let nothing appear great, nothing valuable or admirable, nothing worthy of esteem: nothing high, nothing truly praise-worthy or desirable, but what is eternal.

Let the *eternal truth* please thee above all things, and thy own exceeding great vileness ever displease thee.

Fear nothing so much, blame and abhor nothing so much as thy vices and sins, which ought to displease thee more than any losses whatsoever.

Some persons walk not sincerely before me; but being led with a certain curiosity and pride, desire to know my secrets, and to understand the high things of God, neglecting themselves and their own salvation.

These often fall into great temptations and sins through their pride and curiosity, because I stand against them.

4. Fear the judgments of God, dread the anger of the Almighty; but pretend not to examine the works of the Most High, but search into thy own iniquities, how many ways thou hast offended, and how much good thou hast neglected.

Some only carry their devotion in their books, some in pictures, and some in outward signs and figures.

Some have me in their mouth, but little in their heart.

There are others, who being enlightened in their understanding, and purified in their affections, always breathe after things eternal, are unwilling to hear of earthly things, and grieve to be subject to the necessities of nature; and such as these perceive what the spirit of *truth* speaks in them.

For it teaches them to despise the things of the earth, and to love heavenly things; to neglect the world, and all the day and night to aspire after heaven.

CHAPTER V.
OF THE WONDERFUL EFFECT OF DIVINE LOVE.

1. I Bless thee, O Heavenly Father, Father of my Lord Jesus Christ; because thou hast vouchsafed to be mindful of so poor a wretch as I am.

O Father of mercies, and God of all comfort, I give thanks to thee, who sometimes art pleased to cherish with thy consolations, me that am unworthy of any comfort.

I bless thee and glorify thee evermore, together with thy only begotten Son, and the Holy Ghost the Comforter, to all eternity.

O Lord God, my holy lover, when thou shalt come into my heart, all that is within me will be filled with Joy.

Thou art my glory, and the joy of my heart:

Thou art my hope and my refuge in the day of my tribulation.

2. But because I am as yet weak in love, and imperfect in virtue; therefore do I stand in need to be strengthened and comforted by thee. For this reason visit me often, and instruct me in thy holy discipline.

Free me from evil passions, and heal my heart of all disorderly affections; that being healed and well purged in my interior, I may become fit to love, courageous to suffer, and constant to persevere.

3. Love is an excellent thing, a great good indeed: which alone maketh light all that is burthensome, and equally bears all that is unequal:

For it carries a burthen without being burthened, and makes all that which is bitter sweet and savoury.

The love of Jesus is noble and generous, it spurs us on to do great things, and excites to desire all that which is more perfect.

Love will tend upwards, and not be detained by things beneath.

Love will be at liberty, and free from all worldly affection, lest its interior sight be hindered, lest it suffer itself to be entangled with any temporal interest, or cast down by losses.

Nothing is sweeter than love, nothing stronger, nothing higher, nothing wider, nothing more pleasant, nothing fuller or better in heaven or earth: for love proceeds from God, and cannot rest but in God, above all things created.

4. The lover flies, runs, and rejoices; he is free, and is not held.

He gives all for all, and has all in all; because he rests in one sovereign *good* above all, from whom all good flows and proceeds.

He looks not at the gifts, but turns himself to the giver, above all goods.

Love often knows no measure, but is fervent above all measure.

Love feels no burthen, values no labours, would willingly do more than it can; complains not of impossibility, because it conceives that it may and can do all things.

It is able therefore to do any thing, and it performs and effects many things, where he that loves not faints and lies down.

5. Love watches, and sleeping slumbers not.

When weary, is not tired; when straitened, is not constrained; when frighted, is not disturbed; but like a lively flame, and a torch all on fire, mounts upwards, and securely passes through all opposition.

Whosoever loves knows the cry of this voice.

A loud cry in the ears of God is the ardent affection of the soul, which saith; O my God, my love: thou art all mine, and I am all thine.

6. Give increase to my love, that I may learn to taste with the interior mouth of the heart how sweet it is to love, and to swim, and to be melted in love.

Let me be possessed by love, going above myself through excess of fervour and amazement.

Let me sing the canticle of love, let me follow thee my Beloved on High, let my soul lose herself in thy praises, rejoicing exceedingly in thy love.

Let me love thee more than myself, and myself only for thee: and all others in thee, who truly love thee, as the law of love commands, which shines forth from thee.

7. Love is swift, sincere, pious, pleasant, and delightful; strong, patient, faithful, prudent, long-suffering, courageous, and never seeking itself; for where a man seeks himself, there he falls from love.

Love is circumspect, humble, upright, not soft, not light, nor intent upon vain things; is sober, chaste, stable, quiet, and keeps a guard over all the senses.

Love is submissive and obedient to superiors, in its own eyes mean and contemptible, devout and thankful to God, always trusting and hoping in him, even then when it tastes not the relish of God's sweetness; for there is no living in love without some pain or sorrow.

8. Whosoever is not ready to suffer all things, and to stand resigned to the will of his Beloved, is not worthy to be called a lover.

He that loves must willingly embrace all that is hard and bitter for the sake of his Beloved, and never suffer himself to be turned away from him by any contrary occurrences whatsoever.

CHAPTER VI.
OF THE PROOF OF A TRUE LOVER.

1. My son, thou art not as yet a valiant and prudent lover.

Why, O Lord?

Because thou fallest off from what thou hast begun upon meeting a little adversity, and too greedily seekest after consolation.

A valiant lover stands his ground in temptations, and gives no credit to the crafty persuasions of the enemy.

As he is pleased with me in prosperity, so I displease him not when I send adversity.

2. A prudent lover considers not so much the gift of the lover, as the love of the giver.

He looks more at the good-will than the value, and sets his Beloved above all his gifts.

A generous lover rests not in the gift, but in me above every gift.

All is not lost, if sometimes thou hast not that feeling [of devotion] towards me or my saints, which thou wouldst have.

That good and delightful affection, which thou sometimes perceivest, is the effect of present grace, and a certain foretaste of thy heavenly country.

But thou must not rely too much upon it, because it goes and comes.

But to fight against the evil motions of the mind which arise, and to despise the suggestions of the devil, is a sign of virtue and of great merit.

3. Let not therefore strange fancies trouble thee of what subject soever they be that are suggested to thee.

Keep thy resolution firm, and thy intentions upright towards God.

Neither is it an illusion, that sometimes thou art rapt into an extasy, and presently returnest to the accustomed fooleries of thy heart.

For these thou rather sufferest against thy will, than procurest: and as long as thou art displeased with them, and resistest them, it is merit and not loss.

4. Know, that the old enemy strives by all means to hinder thy desire after good, and to divert thee from every devout exercise; namely, from the veneration of the saints, from the pious meditation of my passion: from the profitable remembrance of thy sins, from keeping a guard upon thy own heart, and from a firm purpose of advancing in virtue.

He suggests to thee many evil thoughts, that he may tire thee out, and fright thee; that he may withdraw thee from prayer, and the reading of devout books.

He is displeased with humble *confession:* and, if he could, he would cause thee to let *communion* alone.

Give no credit to him, value him not, although he often lay his deceitful snares in thy way.

Charge him with it, when he suggests wicked and unclean things: and say to him:

Be gone, unclean spirit; be ashamed miserable wretch; thou art very filthy indeed to suggest such things as these to me.

Depart from me, thou most wicked impostor; thou shalt have no share in me; but my Jesus will be with me as a valiant warrior, and thou shalt stand confounded.

I had rather die, and undergo any torment whatsoever, than consent to thee.

Be silent, I will hear no more of thee, although thou often strive to be troublesome to me.

The Lord is my light, and my salvation: whom shall I fear?

If whole armies should stand together against me, my heart shall not fear. The Lord is my helper, and my Redeemer. Psalms cvi.

5. Fight like a good soldier; and if sometimes thou fall through frailty, rise up again with greater strength than before, confiding in my more abundant grace. But take great care thou yield not to any vain complacence and pride.

Through this many are led into error, and sometimes fall into almost incurable blindness.

Let this fall of the proud, who foolishly presume of themselves, serve thee for a warning, and keep thee always humble.

CHAPTER VII.
THAT GRACE IS TO BE HID UNDER THE GUARDIANSHIP OF HUMILITY.

My Son, it is more and more safe for thee to hide the grace of devotion and not to be elevated with it, not to speak much of it, not to consider it much; but rather to despise thyself the more, and to be afraid of it as given to one unworthy.

Thou must not depend too much on this affection, which may be quickly changed into the contrary.

When thou hast grace, think with thyself how miserable and poor thou art wont to be, when thou art without it.

Nor does the progress of a spiritual life consist so much in having the grace of consolation, as in bearing the want of it with humility, resignation, and patience; so as not to grow remiss in thy exercise of prayer at that time, nor to suffer thyself to omit any of thy accustomed good works.

But that thou willingly do what lies in thee, according to the best of thy ability and understanding; and take care not wholly to neglect thyself through the dryness or anxiety of mind which thou feelest.

2. For there are many, who, when it succeeds not well with them, presently grow impatient or slothful.

Now *the way of man is not always in his own power;* but it belongs to God to give, and to comfort when he will, and as much as he will, and whom he will, as it shall please him, and no more.

Some wanting discretion, have ruined themselves upon occasion of the grace of devotion; because they were for doing more than they could, not weighing well the measure of their own weakness, but following rather the inclination of the heart than the judgment of reason.

And because they presumptuously undertook greater things than were pleasing to God, therefore they quickly lost his grace.

They became needy, and were left in a wretched condition, who had built themselves a nest in heaven; to the end, that being thus humbled and impoverished, they may learn not to trust to their own wings, but to hide themselves under mine.

Those who are as yet but novices and unexperienced in the way of the Lord, if they will not govern themselves by the counsel of the discreet, will easily be deceived and overthrown.

3. And if they will rather follow their own judgment than believe others that have more experience, they will be in danger of coming off ill if they continue to refuse to lay down their own conceits.

They that are wise in their own eyes seldom humbly suffer themselves to be ruled by others.

It is better to have little knowledge with humility, and a weak understanding, than greater treasures of learning with a vain self-complacence.

It is better for thee to have less than much, which may puff thee up with pride.

He is not so discreet as he ought, who gives himself up wholly to joy, forgetting his former poverty, and the chaste fear of God, which apprehends the losing of that grace which is offered.

Neither is he so virtuously wise, who in the time of adversity, or any tribulation whatsoever, carries himself in a desponding way, and conceives and feels less confidence in me than he ought.

4. He, who is too secure in the time of peace, will often be found too much dejected and fearful in the time of war.

If thou couldst always continue humble and little in thy own eyes, and keep thy spirit in due order and subjection, thou wouldst not fall so easily into danger and offence.

It is a good counsel, that when thou hast conceived the spirit of fervour, thou shouldst meditate how it will be with thee when that light shall leave thee.

Which when it shall happen remember that the light may return again, which for a caution to thee, and for my glory, I have withdrawn from thee for a time.

5. Such a trial is oftentimes more profitable than if thou wert always to have prosperity according to thy will.

For a man's merits are not to be estimated by his having many visions of consolations; or by his knowledge of scriptures, or by his being placed in a more elevated station:

But by his being grounded in true humility, and replenished with divine charity: by his seeking always purely and entirety the honour of God; by his esteeming himself to be nothing, and sincerely despising himself; and being better pleased to be despised and humbled by others, than to be honoured by them.

CHAPTER VIII.
OF THE MEAN ESTEEM OF ONE'S SELF IN THE SIGHT OF GOD.

1. I will speak to my Lord, I that am but dust and ashes. Genesis xviii.

If I think any thing better of myself, behold thou standest against me; and my sins bear witness to the truth, and I cannot contradict it.

But if I vilify myself, and acknowledge my own nothing, and cast away all manner of esteem of myself; and, as I really am, account myself to be mere dust, thy grace will be favourable to me, and thy light will draw nigh to my heart, and all self esteem, how small soever, will be sunk in the depth of my own nothingness, and there lose itself for ever.

It is there thou shewest me to myself, what I am, what I have been, and what I am come to: for I am nothing, and I knew it not.

If I am left to myself, behold I am nothing, and all weakness; but if thou suddenly look upon me, I presently become strong, and am filled with a new joy.

And it is very wonderful that I am so quickly raised up, and so graciously embraced by thee; I, who by my own weight am always sinking to the bottom.

2. It is thy love that effects this, freely preventing me, and assisting me in so many necessities; preserving me also from grievous dangers; and, as I may truly say, delivering me from innumerable evils.

For by an evil loving of myself, I lost myself; and by seeking thee alone and purely loving thee, I found both myself and thee, and by this love have more profoundly annihilated myself.

Because thou, O most sweet Lord, dost deal with me above all desert, and above all that I dare hope or ask for.

8. Blessed be thou, O my God; for though I am unworthy of all good, yet thy generosity and infinite goodness never ceaseth to do good even to those that are ungrateful, and that are turned away from thee.

O convert us to thee, that we may be thankful, humble, and devout; for thou art our salvation, our power and our strength.

CHAPTER IX.
THAT ALL THINGS ARE TO BE REFERRED TO GOD, AS TO OUR LAST END.

1. My Son, I must be thy chief and last end, if thou desirest to be truly happy.

By this intention shall thy affections be purified, which too often are irregularly bent upon thyself, and things created.

For if in any thing thou seek thyself, thou presently faintest away within thyself, and growest dry.

Refer therefore all things principally to me, for it is I that have given thee all.

Consider every thing as flowing from the sovereign good: and therefore they must all be returned to me as to their origin.

2. Out of me both little and great, poor and rich, as out of a living fountain, draw living water; and they that freely and willingly serve me shall receive *grace for grace*.

But he that would glory in any thing else besides me, or delight in any good as his own [not referred to me] shall not be established in true joy, nor enlarged in his heart, but in many kinds shall meet with hindrances and anguish:

Therefore thou must not ascribe any thing of good to thyself, nor attribute virtue to any man; but give all to God, without whom man has nothing.

I have given all, I will have all returned to me again, and I very strictly require thanks for all that I give.

3. This is that *truth*, by which all *vain glory* is put to flight:

And if heavenly grace and true charity come in, there shall be no envy nor narrowness of heart, nor shall self-love keep its hold.

For divine charity overcomes all, and dilates all the forces of the soul.

If thou art truly wise, thou wilt rejoice in me alone, thou wilt hope in me alone: for *none is good but God alone*, (Luke xviii.) who is to be praised above all, and to be blessed in all.

CHAPTER X.
THAT IT IS MEET TO SERVE GOD, DESPISING THIS WORLD.

1. Now will I speak, O Lord, and will not be silent; I will say in the hearing of my God, my Lord, and my king that is on high.

O how great is the multitude of thy sweetness, O Lord, which thou hast hidden for those that fear thee! Psalms xxx. [USCCB: Psalms xxxi. 20.]

But what art thou to those that love thee? What to those that serve thee with their whole heart?

Unspeakable indeed is the sweetness of thy contemplation, which thou bestowest on those that love thee.

In this, most of all hast thou shewed me the sweetness of thy love, that when I had no being, thou hast made me; and when I strayed far from thee, thou hast brought me back again, that I might serve thee; and thou hast commanded me to *love* thee.

2. O fountain of everlasting *love*, what shall I say of thee?

How can I ever forget thee, who hast vouchsafed to remember me, even after that I was laid waste, and perished?

Thou hast beyond all hope shewed mercy to thy servant; and beyond all my desert bestowed thy grace and friendship on me.

What return shall I make to thee for this grace? for it is a favour not granted to all, to forsake all things and renounce the world, and chuse a monastic life.

Can it be much to serve thee, whom the whole creation is bound to serve?

It ought not to seem much to me to serve thee; but this seems great and wonderful to me, that thou vouchsafest to receive one so wretched and unworthy into thy service, and to associate him to thy beloved servants.

3. Behold all things are thine, which I have, and with which I serve thee;

Though rather thou servest me, than I thee.

Lo! heaven and earth, which thou hast created for the service of man, are ready at thy beck, and daily do whatever thou hast commanded them.

And this is yet but little, for thou hast also appointed the angels for the service of man.

But, what is above all this is, that thou thyself hast vouchsafed to serve man, and hast promised that thou wilt give him thyself.

4. What shall I give thee for all these thousands of favours? Oh that I could serve thee all the days of my life!

Oh that I were able, if it were but for one day, to serve thee worthily!

Indeed thou art worthy of all service, of all honour, and of eternal praise.

Thou art truly my Lord, and I am thy poor servant, who am bound with all my strength to serve thee, and ought never to grow weary of praising thee.

This is my will, this is my desire; and whatever is wanting to me, do thou vouchsafe to supply.

5. It is a great honour, a great glory to serve thee, and to despise all things for thee;

For they who willingly subject themselves to thy most holy service shall have a great grace;

They shall find the most sweet consolation of the Holy Ghost, who for the love of thee have cast away all carnal delight:

They shall gain great freedom of mind, who for thy name enter upon the narrow way, and neglect all worldly care.

6. Oh pleasant and delightful **service** of God, which makes a man truly free and holy!

O sacred state of religious bondage, which makes man equal to angels, pleasing to God, terrible to the devils, and commendable to all the faithful!

Oh service worthy to be embraced and always wished for, which leads to the supreme good, and procures a joy that will never end.

CHAPTER XI.
THAT THE DESIRES OF OUR HEART ARE TO BE EXAMINED AND MODERATED.

1. Son, thou hast many things still to learn, which thou hast not yet well learned.

What are these things, O Lord?

That thou conform in all things thy desire to my good pleasure, and that thou be not a lover of thyself, but earnestly zealous that my will may be done.

Desires often inflame thee, and violently hurry thee on; but consider whether it be for my honour, or thy own interest that thou art more moved.

If thou hast no other view but me, thou wilt be well contented with whatever I shall ordain; but if there lurk in thee any thing of self-seeking, behold this is it that hinders thee, and troubles thee.

2. Take care then not to rely too much upon any desire which thou hast conceived before thou hast consulted me, lest afterwards thou repent, or be displeased with that which before pleased thee, and which thou zealously desiredst as the best.

For every affection [or inclination] which appears good, is not presently to be followed, nor every contrary affection at the first to be rejected.

Even in good desires and inclinations, it is expedient sometimes to use some restraint, lest by too much eagerness, thou incur distraction of mind; lest thou create scandal to others, by not keeping within discipline; or by the opposition which thou mayest meet with from others, thou be suddenly disturbed and fall.

3. Yet in some cases we must use violence, and manfully resist the sensual appetite, and not regard what the flesh has a mind for, or what it would fly from; but rather labour that, whether it will or no, it may become subject to the spirit.

And so long must it be chastised, and kept under servitude, till it readily obey in all things, and learn to be content with a little, and to be pleased with what is plain and ordinary, and not to murmur at any inconvenience.

CHAPTER XII.
OF LEARNING PATIENCE, AND OF FIGHTING AGAINST CONCUPISCENCE.

1. O Lord God, patience, as I perceive, is very necessary for me; this life is exposed to many adversities:

For howsoever I propose for my peace, my life cannot be without war and sorrow.

2. So It is, Son; but I would not have thee seek for such a peace as to be without temptations, or to meet with no adversities.

But even then to think thou hast found peace, when thou shalt be exercised with divers tribulations, and tried in many adversities.

If thou shalt say, thou art not able to suffer so much, how then wilt thou endure the fire of purgatory?

Of two evils one ought always to choose the least.

That thou mayest therefore escape the everlasting punishments to come, labour to endure present evils with patience for God's sake.

Dost thou think the men of the world suffer little or nothing? Thou shalt not find it so, though thou seek out for the most delicate.

5. But, thou wilt say they have many delights, and follow their own wills; and therefore make small account of their tribulations.

4. Suppose it to be so, that they have all they desire: how long dost thou think this will last?

Behold, they shall vanish away like smoke that abound in this world, and there shall be no remembrance of their past joys.

Nay, even whilst they are living, they rest not in them, without bitterness, irksomeness, and fear.

For the very same thing, in which they conceive a delight, doth often bring upon them the punishment of sorrow.

It is just it should be so with them, that since they inordinately seek and follow their pleasures, they should not satisfy them without confusion and uneasiness.

Oh! how short, how deceitful, how inordinate and filthy, are all these pleasures!

Yet through sottishness and blindness men understand this not; but like brute beasts, for a small pleasure in this mortal life, they incur the eternal death of their souls.

But thou, my son, Go not after thy concupiscences, but turn away from thy own will. Ecclesiastes xviii.

[USCCB: Sirach xviii. 30.]

Delight in the Lord, and he will give thee the requests of thy heart. Psalms xxxvi.

[USCCB: Psalms xxxvii. 4.]

5. For if thou wilt be delighted in truth, and receive more abundant consolation from me, behold it is in the contempt of all worldly things: and the renouncing all those mean pleasures shall be thy blessing, and an exceeding great comfort to thy soul.

And the more thou withdrawest thyself from all comfort from things created, the more sweet and the more powerful consolation shalt thou find in me.

But thou shalt not at first attain to these without some sorrow and labor in the conflict.

The old custom will stand in thy way, but by a better custom it shall be overcome.

The flesh will complain, but by the fervour of the spirit it shall be kept under.

The old serpent will tempt thee and give thee trouble; but by prayer he shall be put to flight: moreover, by keeping thyself always employed in some useful labour, his access to thee shall be in a great measure stopt up.

CHAPTER XIII.
OF THE OBEDIENCE OF AN HUMBLE SUBJECT AFTER THE EXAMPLE OF JESUS CHRIST.

1. Son, he who strives to withdraw himself from obedience, withdraws himself from grace; and he that seeks to have things for his own particular, loses such as are common.

If a man doth not freely and willingly submit himself to his superiors, it is a sign that his flesh is not as yet perfectly obedient to him; but oftentimes rebels and murmurs.

Learn then to submit thyself readily to thy superior, if thou desire to subdue thy own flesh;

For the enemy without is sooner overcome, if the inward man be not laid waste.

There is no more troublesome or worse enemy to the soul than thou art to thyself, not agreeing well with the spirit.

Thou must in good earnest conceive a true contempt of thyself, if thou wilt prevail over flesh and blood.

Because thou yet hast too inordinate a love for thyself, therefore art thou afraid to resign thyself wholly to the will of others.

2. But what great matter is it, if thou, who art but dust and a mere nothing, submittest thyself for God's sake to man; when I the **Almighty**, and the **Most High**, who created all things out of nothing, have for thy sake humbly subjected myself to man.

I became the most humble and most abject of all men, that thou mightest overcome thy pride by my humility.

Learn, O dust, to obey, learn to humble thyself thou that art but dirt and mire, and to cast thyself down under the feet of all men.

Learn to break thy own will, and to yield thyself up to all subjection.

3. Conceive an indignation against thyself, suffer not the swelling of pride to live in thee: but make thyself so submissive and little, that all may trample on thee, and tread thee under their feet, as the dirt of the streets.

What hast thou, vain man, to complain of?

What answer canst thou make, O filthy sinner, to those that reproach thee, thou that hast so often offended God, and many times deserved hell?

But mine eye hath spared thee, because thy soul was precious in my sight, that thou mightest know my love, and mightest be always thankful for my favours, and that thou mightest give thyself continually to true subjection and humility; and bear with patience to be despised by all.

CHAPTER XIV.
OF CONSIDERING THE SECRET JUDGMENTS OF GOD, LEST WE BE PUFFED UP BY OUR GOOD WORKS.

1. Thou thunderest forth over my head thy judgments, O Lord, and thou shakest all my bones with fear and trembling, and my soul is terrified exceedingly.

I stand astonished, and consider that the *heavens are not pure in thy sight*.

If in the angels thou hast found sin, and hast not spared them, what will become of me?

Stars have fallen from heaven, and I that am but dust, how can I presume?

They, whose works seemed praiseworthy, have fallen to the very lowest; and such as before fed upon the bread of angels, I have seen delighted with the husks of swine.

2. There is then no sanctity, if thou O Lord, withdraw thy hand:

No wisdom avails, if thou cease to govern us:

No strength is of any help, if thou support us not:

No chastity is secure without thy protection:

No guard that we can keep upon ourselves profits us, if thy holy watchfulness be not with us:

For it we are left to ourselves, we sink and we perish; but if thou visit us, we are raised up and we live.

For we are unsettled, but by thee we are strengthened: we are tepid, but by thee we are inflamed.

3. O how humbly and lowly ought I to think of myself! how little ought I to esteem whatever good I may seem to have?

Oh! how low ought I to cast myself down under the bottomless depth of thy judgments, O Lord, where I find myself to be *nothing* else but *nothing* and *nothing?*

Oh! immense weight! Oh! sea, that cannot be passed over, where I find nothing of myself but just nothing at all.

Where then can there be any lurking hole for glorying in myself? where any confidence in any conceit of my own virtue?

All vain-glory is swallowed up in the depth of thy judgments over me.

4. What is all flesh in thy sight? shall the clay glory against him that formed it?

How can he be puffed up with the vain talk of man, whose heart in *truth* is subjected to God.

All the world will not lift him up, whom *truth* hath subjected to itself:

Neither will he be moved with the tongues of all that praise him, who hath settled his whole hope in God.

For behold, they also that speak are all *nothing*, for they shall pass away with the sound of their words; but *the truth of the Lord remaineth for ever*. Psalms cxiv.

CHAPTER XV.
HOW WE ARE TO BE DISPOSED, AND WHAT WE ARE TO SAY WHEN WE DESIRE ANY THING.

1. My Son, say thus in every occasion; Lord, if it be pleasing to thee, let this be done in this manner.

Lord, if it be to thy honour, let this be done in thy name.

Lord, if thou seest that this is expedient, and approvest it as profitable for me, then grant that I may use it to thy honour;

But if thou knowest that it will be hurtful to me, and not expedient for the salvation of my soul, take away from me such a desire.

For every desire is not from the Holy Ghost, though it seem to a man right and good.

And it is hard to judge truly, whether it be a good or bad spirit that pushes thee on to desire this, or that, or whether thou art not moved to it by thy own spirit.

Many in the end have been deceived, who at first seemed to be led by a good spirit.

2. Whatsoever therefore presents itself to thy mind as worthy to be desired; see that it is always with the fear of God, and the humility of heart that thou desire or ask for it;

And above all, thou oughtest with a resignation of thyself to commit all to me, and to say,

O Lord, thou knowest what is best; let this or that be done as thou wilt.

Give what thou wilt, how much thou wilt, and at what time thou wilt.

Do with me as thou knowest, and as best pleaseth thee, and is most for thy honour.

Put me where thou wilt, and do with me in all things according to thy will.

I am in thy hand, turn me round which way thou wilt.

Lo, I am thy servant, ready to obey thee in all things; for I dont desire to live for myself, but for thee: I wish it may be perfectly and worthily.

A Prayer

For the fulfilling of the Will of God.

3. Grant me thy grace, most merciful Jesus, that it may be with me, and may labour with me, and continue with me to the end.

Grant me always to will and desire that which is most acceptable to thee, and which pleaseth thee best.

Let thy will be mine, and let my will always follow thine, and agree perfectly with it.

Let me always will or not will the same with thee; and let me not be able to will or not will any otherwise than as thou willest or willest not.

4. Grant that I may die to all things that are in the world; and for thy sake love to be despised, and not to be known in this world.

Grant that I may rest, in thee above all things desired, and that my heart may be at peace in thee.

Thou art the true peace of the heart, thou art its only rest; out of thee all things are hard and uneasy.

In this ***peace, in the self same*** (that is, in Thee, the one sovereign eternal Good) *I will sleep and take my rest*. (Psalms iv.) **Amen**.

CHAPTER XVI.
THAT TRUE COMFORT IS TO BE SOUGHT IN GOD ALONE.

1. Whatsoever I can desire or imagine for my comfort, I look not for it in this life, but hereafter.

For if I alone should have all the comforts of this world, and might enjoy all its delights, it is certain they could not last long.

Wherefore thou canst not, O my soul, be fully comforted, nor perfectly delighted, but in God, the comforter of the poor, and the support of the humble.

Expect a little while, my soul, wait for the divine promise, and thou shalt have plenty of all that is good in heaven.

If thou desirest too inordinately these present things, thou wilt lose those that are heavenly and everlasting.

Let temporal things serve thy use, but the eternal be the object of thy desire.

Thou canst not be fully satisfied with any temporal good, because thou wast not created for the enjoyment of such things.

2. Although thou shouldst have all created goods, yet this could not make thee happy and blessed: but in God, who created all things, all thy beatitude and happiness consists.

Not such a happiness as is seen or cried up by the foolish admirers of this world, but such as good Christians look for, and of which they that are spiritual and clean of heart, whose conversation is in heaven, have sometimes a foretaste.

All human comfort is vain and short.

Blessed and true is that comfort which is inwardly received from **truth**.

A devout man always carrieth about with him Jesus his Comforter, and saith to him, be with me, O Lord Jesus, in all places, and at all times.

Let this be my consolation, to be willing to want all human comfort.

And if thy comfort also be withdrawn, let thy will, and just appointment for my trial be to me as the greatest of comforts.

For thou wilt not always be angry, nor wilt thou threaten for ever. Psalms cii.

CHAPTER XVII.
THAT WE OUGHT TO CAST ALL OUR CARE UPON GOD.

1. Son, suffer me to do with thee what I will: I know what is best for thee:

Thou thinkest as man: thou judgest in many things as human affection suggests.

Lord, what thou sayest is true, thy care over me is greater than all the care I can take of myself.

For he stands at too great a hazard that does not cast his whole care on thee.

Lord, provided that my will remain but firm towards thee, do with me whatsoever it shall please thee:

For it cannot but be good whatever thou shalt do by me.

2. If thou wilt have me to be in darkness, be thou blessed; and if thou wilt have me to be in light, be thou again blessed. If thou vouchsafe to comfort me, be thou blessed: and if it be thy will that I should be afflicted, be thou always equally blessed.

3. Son, it is in this manner thou must stand affected, if thou desire to walk with me.

Thou must be as ready to suffer as to rejoice; thou must be as willing to be poor and needy, as to be full and rich.

4. Lord, I will suffer willingly for thee whatsoever thou art pleased should befal me.

I will receive with indifference from thy hand good and evil, sweet and bitter, joyful and sorrowful; and will give thee thanks for all that happens to me.

Keep me only from all sin, and I will fear neither death nor hell.

Cast me not off for ever, nor blot me out of the book of life; and what tribulation soever befalleth me shall not hurt me.

CHAPTER XVIII.
THAT TEMPORAL MISERIES ARE TO BE BORNE WITH PATIENCE AFTER THE EXAMPLE OF JESUS CHRIST.

1. Son, I came down from heaven for thy salvation, I took upon me thy miseries, not of necessity, but moved thereto by charity, that thou mightest learn patience, and mightest bear without repining the miseries of this life:

For from the hour of my birth, till my expiring on the cross, I was never without suffering.

I underwent a great want of temporal things; I frequently heard many complaints against me; I meekly bore with confusions and reproaches.

For my benefits I received ingratitude; for my miracles, blasphemies; and for my heavenly doctrine, reproaches.

2. Lord, because thou wast patient in thy life-time, in this chiefly fulfilling the commandment of thy Father, it is fitting that I a wretched sinner should, according to thy will, take all with patience; and as long as thou pleasest, support the burden of this corruptible life, in order to my salvation.

For though this present life be burthensome, yet it is become through thy grace, meritorious; and by the help of thy example, and the footsteps of thy saints, more supportable to the weak, and more lightsome.

It is also much more comfortable, than it was formerly under the old law, when the gate of heaven remained shut; and the way to heaven seemed more obscure, when so few concerned themselves to seek the kingdom of heaven.

Neither could they who were then just, and to be saved, enter into thy heavenly kingdom, before thy passion, and the payment of our debt by thy sacred death.

3. Oh! how great thanks am I obliged to return thee, for having vouchsafed to shew me and all the faithful, a right and good way to an everlasting kingdom!

For thy life is our way; and by holy patience we walk on to thee, who art our crown.

If thou hadst not gone before and instructed us, who would have cared to have followed?

Alas! how many would have staid afar off, and a great way behind, if they had not before their eyes thy excellent example?

Behold we are still tepid, notwithstanding all thy miracles and instructions which we have heard: what then would it have been, if we had not this great light to follow thee?

CHAPTER XIX.
OF SUPPORTING INJURIES; AND WHO IS PROVED TO BE TRULY PATIENT.

1. What is it thou sayest, my Son? Cease to complain, considering my passion, and that of other saints:

Thou hast not yet resisted unto blood:

What thou sufferedst is but little, in comparison of them who have suffered so much; who have been so strongly tempted, so grievously afflicted, so many ways tried and exercised.

Thou must then call to mind the heavy sufferings of others, that thou mayest the easier bear the little things thou sufferest.

And if to thee they seemed not little, take heed lest this also proceed from thy impatience.

But whether they be little or great, strive to bear them all with patience.

2. The better thou disposest thyself to sufferings, the more wisely dost thou act, and the more dost thou merit; and thou wilt bear it more easily, thy mind being well prepared for it, and accustomed to it.

Do not say, I cannot take these things from such a man, and things of this kind are not to be suffered by me, for he has done me a great injury, and he upbraids me with things I never thought on; but I will suffer willingly from another, and as far as I shall judge fitting for me to suffer.

Such a thought is foolish, which considers not the virtue of patience, nor by whom it shall be crowned; but rather weighs the persons, and the offences committed.

3. He is not a true patient man, who will suffer no more than he thinks good, and from whom he pleaseth.

The true patient man minds not by whom it is he is exercised, whether by his superior, or by one of his equals, or by an inferior; whether by a good and holy man, or one that is perverse and unworthy.

But how much soever, and how often soever any adversity happens to him from any thing created, he takes it all with equality of mind as from the hand of God, with thanksgiving, and esteems it a great gain.

For nothing, how little soever, that is suffered for God's sake, can pass without merit in the sight of God.

4. Be thou therefore ready prepared to fight, if thou desirest to gain the victory.

Without fighting thou cannot obtain the crown of patience.

If thou wilt not suffer, thou refusest to be crowned; but if thou desirest to be crowned, fight manfully and endure patiently.

Without labour there is no coming to rest, nor without fighting can the victory be obtained.

May thy grace, O Lord, make that possible to me, which seems impossible to me by nature.

Thou knowest that I can bear but little, and that I am quickly cast down by a small adversity.

Let all exercises of tribulation become amiable and agreeable to me for thy name's sake; for to suffer and to be afflicted for thee is very healthful for my soul.

CHAPTER XX.
OF THE CONFESSION OF OUR INFIRMITY, AND OF THE MISERIES OF THIS LIFE.

1. *I will confess against myself my injustice*. Psalms xxxi. I will confess to thee, O Lord, my infirmity.

It is oftentimes a small thing which casts me down and troubles me.

I make a resolution to behave myself valiantly; but when a small temptation comes, I am brought into great straits.

It is sometimes a very trifling thing, from whence a grievous temptation proceeds.

And when I think myself somewhat safe, I find myself sometimes, when I least apprehend it, almost overcome with a small blast.

2. Behold, then, O Lord, my abjection and frailty every way known to thee.

Have pity on me, and draw me out of the mire, that I stick not fast therein, that I may not be utterly cast down for ever.

This it is which often drives me back, and confounds me in thy sight, to find that I am so subject to fall, and have so little strength to resist my passions.

And although I do not altogether consent, yet their assaults are troublesome and grievous to me; and it is exceedingly irksome to live thus always in a conflict.

From hence my infirmity is made known to me; because wicked thoughts do always much more easily rush in upon me, than they can be cast out again.

3. Oh! that thou the most mighty God of *Israel*, the zealous lover of faithful souls, wouldst behold the labour and sorrow of thy servant, and stand by me in all my undertakings.

Strengthen me with heavenly fortitude, lest the old man, the miserable flesh not yet fully subject to the spirit, prevail and get the upper hand; against which we must fight as long as we breathe in this most wretched life.

Alas! what kind of life is this, where afflictions and miseries are never wanting, where all things are full of snares and enemies.

For when one tribulation or temptation is gone, another cometh; yea, and whilst the first conflict still lasts, many others come on, and those unexpected.

4. And how can a life be loved that hath so great bitterness, that is subject to so many calamities and miseries.

And how can it be called life, since it begets so many deaths and plagues?

And yet it is loved, and many seek their delight in it.

Many blame the world that it is deceitful and vain, and yet they are not willing to quit it, because the concupiscences of the flesh too much prevail.

But there are some things that draw them to love the world, others to despise it.

The lust of the flesh, the lust of the eyes, and pride of life draw to the love of the world; but the pains and miseries which justly follow these things breed a hatred and loathing of the world.

5. But alas! the pleasure of sin prevails over the worldly soul, and under these thorns she imagines there are delights; because she has neither seen nor tasted the sweetness of God, nor the internal pleasure of virtue.

But they that perfectly despise the world, and study to live to God under holy discipline, experience the divine sweetness, that is promised to those who forsake all; and such clearly see how grievously the world is mistaken, and how many ways it is imposed upon.

CHAPTER XXI.
THAT WE ARE TO REST IN GOD ABOVE ALL GOODS AND GIFTS.

1. Above all things, and in all things, do thou my soul rest always in the Lord, for he is the eternal rest of the saints.

Give me, O most sweet and loving Jesus, to repose in thee above all things created, above all health and beauty, above all glory and honour, above all power and dignity, above all knowledge and subtlety, above all riches and arts, above all joy and gladness, above all fame and praise, above all sweetness and consolation, above all hope and promise, above all merit and desire.

Above all gifts and presents that thou canst give and infuse, above all joy and jubilation that the mind can contain or feel; in line, above angels and archangels, and all the host of heaven; above all things visible and invisible, and above all that which thou, my God, art not.

2. For thou, O Lord my God, art the best above all things: thou alone most high, thou alone most powerful; thou alone most sufficient, and most full; thou alone most sweet, and most comfortable:

Thou alone most beautiful, and most loving; thou alone most noble, and most glorious above all things; in whom all good things are found together in all their perfection, and always have been, and always will be.

And therefore whatever thou bestowest upon me, that is not thyself, or whatever thou revealest to me concerning thyself, or promised, as long as I see thee not, nor fully enjoy thee, is too little and insufficient.

Because indeed my heart cannot truly rest, nor be entirely contented, till it rest in thee, and rise above all things created.

3. O my most beloved spouse, Christ Jesus, most pure lover, Lord of the whole creation; who will give me the wings of true liberty, to fly and repose in thee? Oh! when shall it be fully granted me to attend at leisure and see how sweet thou art, O Lord my God.

When shall I fully recollect myself in thee, that through the love of thee I may not feel myself, but thee alone, above all feeling and measure, in a manner not known to all?

But now I often sigh, and bear my misfortune with grief;

Because I meet with many evils in this vale of miseries, which frequently disturb me, afflict me, and cast a cloud over me: often hinder me and distract me, allure and entangle me, that I cannot have free access to thee, nor enjoy thy sweet embraces, which are ever enjoyed by blessed spirits.

Let my sighs move thee, and this manifold desolation under which I labour upon earth.

4. O Jesus, the brightness of eternal glory, the comfort of a soul in its pilgrimage; with thee is my mouth without voice, and my silence speaks to thee.

How long doth my Lord delay to come. Let him come to me, his poor servant, and make me joyful: let him stretch forth his hand, and deliver me a wretch from all anguish.

O come, O come; for without thee I can never have one joyful day nor hour, for thou art my joy; and without thee my table is empty.

I am miserable, and in a manner imprisoned, and loaded with fetters, till thou comfort me with the light of thy presence, and restore me to liberty, and shew me a favourable countenance.

5. Let others seek instead of thee whatever else they please; nothing else doth please me, or shall please me, but thou my God, my hope, my eternal salvation.

I will not hold my peace, nor cease to pray till thy grace returns, and thou speak to me interiorly.

6. Behold here I am; behold I come to thee, because thou hast called upon me.

Thy tears, and the desire of thy soul, thy humiliation and contrition of heart have inclined and brought me to thee.

7. And I said, O Lord, I have called upon thee, and have desired to enjoy thee, and am ready to renounce all other things for thee.

For thou didst first stir me up that I might seek thee.

Be thou therefore blessed, O Lord, who hath shewed this goodness to thy servant, according to the multitude of thy mercies.

What hath thy servant more to say in thy presence, but to humble himself exceedingly before thee; always remembering his own iniquity and vileness.

For there is none like to thee, amongst all things that are wonderful in heaven or earth.

Thy works are exceedingly good, thy judgments are true, and by thy providence all things are ruled.

Praise therefore and glory be to thee, O Wisdom of the Father: let my tongue, my soul, and all things created join in praising thee, and blessing thee.

CHAPTER XXII.
OF THE REMEMBERANCE OF THE MANIFOLD BENEFITS OF GOD.

1. Open, O Lord, my heart in thy law, and teach me to walk in thy commandments.

Give me grace to understand thy will, and to commemorate with great reverence and diligent consideration all thy benefits, as well in general as in particular, that so I may be able worthily to give thee thanks for them.

But I know and confess that I am not able to return thee thanks, not even for the least point.

I am less than any of thy benefits bestowed upon me; and when I consider thy excellency, my spirit loses itself in the greatness of thy Majesty.

2. All that we have in soul and body, all that we possess outwardly or inwardly, by nature or grace, are thy benefits, and commend thy bounty, mercy and goodness, from whom we have received all good.

And though one has received more, another less, yet all is thine, and without thee even the least cannot be had.

He that has received greater things cannot glory of his own merit, nor extol himself above others, nor insult over the lesser; because he is indeed greater and better, who attributes less to himself, and is more humble and devout in returning thanks.

And he who esteems himself the vilest of all men, and judges himself the most unworthy, is fittest to receive the greatest blessings.

3. But he that has received fewer must not be troubled, nor take it ill, nor envy him that is more enriched; but attend rather to thee, and very much praise thy goodness, for that thou bestowest thy gifts so plentifully, so freely and willingly without respect of persons.

All things are from thee, and therefore thou art to be praised in all.

Thou knowest what is fit to be given to every one; and why this person hath less, and the other more, is not our business to decide, but thine, who keepest an exact account of the merits of each one.

4. Wherefore, O Lord God, I take it for a great benefit, not to have much which outwardly and according to men might appear praise-worthy and glorious. So that a person, considering his own poverty and meanness, ought not upon that account to be weighed down, or to be grieved and dejected, but rather to receive comfort and great pleasure.

Because thou, O God, hast chosen the poor and the humble, and those that are despised by this world, for thy familiar friends and domestics.

Witness thy apostles themselves, whom thou hast appointed rulers over all the earth.

And yet they conversed in this world without complaint, so humble and simple, without any malice or guile, that they were even glad when they suffered affronts and reproaches for thy name; and what the world flies from, they embraced with great affection.

5. Nothing therefore ought to give so great joy to him that loves thee, and knows thy benefits, and the accomplishment of thy will in himself, and the pleasure of thy eternal appointment.

With which he ought to be so far contented and comforted, as to be willing to be the least, as any one would wish to be the greatest, and to enjoy as much peace and content in the lowest place, as in the highest; and to be as willing to be despicable and mean, and of no name and repute in the world, as to be preferred in honour, and greater than others:

For thy will, and the love of thy honour, ought to be regarded above all, and to comfort and please him more than any benefits whatsoever which he hath received, or can receive.

CHAPTER XXIII.
OF FOUR THINGS WHICH BRING MUCH PEACE.

1. Son, I will teach thee now the way of peace and true liberty.

2. Do, Lord; I beseech thee, as thou sayest, for I shall be very glad to hear it.

3. Endeavour, my Son, rather to do the will of another, than thy own.

Ever choose rather to have less, than more.

Always seek the lowest place, and to be inferior to every one.

Always wish and pray that the will of God may be entirely fulfilled in thee.

Behold, such a man as this enters upon the coast of peace and rest.

4. Lord, this thy short speech contains much perfection.

It is short in words, but full in sense, and plentiful in its fruit;

For if it could be faithfully observed by me, I should not be so easily troubled.

For as often as I find myself disquieted and disturbed, I am sensible it is because I have strayed from this doctrine.

But thou, O Lord, who canst do all things, and always lovest the progress of the soul, increase in me thy grace, that I may accomplish this thy word, and perfect my salvation.

A Prayer

Against evil thoughts.

5. O Lord, my God, depart not far from me: O my God, have regard to help me, for divers evil thoughts have risen up against me, and great fears afflicting my soul.

How shall I pass without hurt? How shall I break through them?

6. I (saith he) will go before thee, end will humble the great ones of the earth. Isaiah xxv.

I will open the gates of the prison, and reveal to thee the hidden secrets.

7. Do, Lord, as thou sayest, and let all these wicked thoughts flee from before thy face.

This is my hope and my only comfort, to fly to thee in all tribulations, to confide in thee, to call on thee from my heart, and patiently to look for thy consolation.

Prayer

For the enlightening the Mind.

8. Enlighten me, O good Jesus, with the brightness of the internal light; and cast out all darkness from the dwelling of my heart.

Restrain my many wandering thoughts, and suppress the temptations that violently assault me.

Fight strongly for me, and overcome those wicked beasts, I mean, these alluring concupiscences; that peace may be made in thy power, and the abundance of thy praise may resound in thy holy court, which is a clean conscience.

Command the winds and storms: say to the sea be thou still, and to the north wind, blow thou not; and a great calm shall ensue.

9. Send forth thy light and thy truth, that they may shine upon the earth; for I am an earth that is empty and void, till thou enlightenest me. *Genesis* i.

Pour forth thy grace from above; water my heart with the dew of heaven; send down the waters of devotion, to wash the face of the earth, to bring forth good and perfect fruit.

Lift up my mind, oppressed with the load of sins, and raise my whole desire towards heavenly things; that having tasted the sweetness of the happiness above, I may have no pleasure in thinking of the things of the earth.

10. Draw me away, and deliver me from all unstable comfort of creatures, for no created thing can fully quiet and satisfy my desire.

Join me to thyself with an inseparable bond of love; for thou alone canst satisfy the lover; and without thee all other things are frivolous.

CHAPTER XXIV.
THAT WE ARE NOT TO BE CURIOUS IN ENQUIRING INTO THE LIFE OF OTHERS.

1. Son, be not curious, and give not way to useless cares.

What is this or that to thee? do thou follow me.

For what is it to thee whether this man be such, or such; or that man do or say this, or the other?

Thou art not to answer for others, but must give an account for thyself; why therefore dost thou meddle with them?

Behold, I know every one, and see all things that are done under the sun; and I know how it is with every one, what he thinks, what he would have, and at what his intention aims.

All things therefore are to be committed to me; but as for thy part, keep thyself in good peace, and let the busybody be as busy as he will.

Whatsoever he shall do or say, will come upon himself, because he cannot deceive me.

2. Be not solicitous for the shadow of a great name, neither seek to be familiarly acquainted with many, nor to be particularly loved by men.

For these things beget distractions and great darkness in the heart.

I would willingly speak my word to thee, and reveal my secrets to thee; if thou wouldst diligently observe my coming, and open to me the door of thy heart.

Be careful and watch in prayers, and humble thyself in all things.

CHAPTER XXV.
IN WHAT THINGS THE FIRM PEACE OF THE HEART AND TRUE PROGRESS DOTH CONSIST.

1. Son, I have said, Peace I leave to you, my peace I give to you: not as the world giveth, do I give to you. John xiv.

Peace is what all desire; but all care not for those things which appertain to true *peace*.

My *peace* is with the humble and meek of heart: thy peace shall be in much patience.

If thou wilt hear me, and follow my voice, thou mayest enjoy much *peace*.

2. What then shall I do. Lord?

3. In every thing attend to thyself, what thou art doing, and what thou art saying; and direct thy whole intention to this, that thou mayest please me alone, and neither desire nor seek any thing out of me.

And as for the sayings or doings of others, judge of nothing rashly; neither busy thyself with things not committed to thy care; and thus may it be brought about that thou shalt be little or seldom disturbed.

But never to feel any trouble at all, nor to suffer a grief of heart or body, is not the state of this present life, but of everlasting rest.

Think not therefore that thou hast found true peace, if thou feelest no burden; nor that then all is well, if thou have no adversary; nor that thou hast attained to perfection, if all things be done according to thy inclination.

Neither do thou then conceive a great notion of thyself, or imagine thyself especially beloved, if thou be in great devotion and sweetness: for it is not in such things as these that a true lover of virtue is known; nor doth the progress and perfection of a man consist in these things.

4. In what then, O Lord?

5. In offering thyself with thy whole heart to the will of God; not seeking the things that are thine either in little or great, either in time or eternity.

So that with the same equal countenance thou continue giving thanks both in prosperity and adversity, weighing all things in an equal balance.

If thou come to be so valiant, and long suffering in hope, that when interior comfort is withdrawn, thou canst prepare thy heart to suffer still more; and dost not justify thyself, as if thou oughtest not to suffer such great things; but acknowledgest my justice in all my appointments, and praisest my holy name; then it is that thou walkest in the true and right way of peace, and mayest hope without any question to see my face again with great joy.

And if thou arrive at an entire contempt of thyself, know that then thou shalt enjoy an abundance of peace, as much as is possible in this state of banishment.

CHAPTER XXVI.
OF THE EMINENCE OF A FREE MIND, WHICH HUMBLE PRAYER BETTER PROCURES THAN READING.

1. Lord, this is the work of a perfect man, never to let one's mind slacken from attending to heavenly things, and to pass through many cares, as it were without care; not after the manner of an indolent person, but by a certain prerogative of a free mind, which doth not cleave by an inordinate affection to any thing created.

2. Preserve me, I beseech thee, O my most merciful God, from the cares of this life, that I be not too much entangled by them; from the many necessities of the body, that I may not be ensnared by pleasure; and from all hinderances of the soul, lest being overcome by troubles I be cast down.

I do not say from those things which worldly vanity covets with so much eagerness; but from these miseries, which by the general curse of our mortality, as punishments, weigh down and keep back the soul of thy servant from being able, when it will, to enter into liberty of spirit.

3. O my God, who art unspeakable sweetness, turn into bitterness to me all carnal comfort, which withdraws me from the love of things eternal, and wickedly allures me to itself, by setting before me a certain present delightful good.

O my God, let not flesh and blood prevail over me, let it not overcome me: let not the world and its transitory glory deceive me: let not the devil supplant me by his craft.

Give me fortitude, that I may stand my ground, patience that I may endure, and constancy that I may persevere.

Give me, in lieu of all the comforts of this world, the most delightful unction of thy spirit; and instead of carnal love, infuse into me the love of thy name.

4. Behold! eating, drinking, cloathing, and other necessaries appertaining to the support of the body are burthensome to a fervent spirit.

Grant that I may use such things with moderation, and not be entangled with an inordinate affection to them.

It is not lawful to cast them all away, for nature must be supported; but to require superfluities, and such things as are more delightful, thy holy law forbids; for otherwise the flesh would grow insolent against the spirit.

In all this, I beseech thee, let thy hand govern and direct me, that I may no way exceed.

CHAPTER XXVII.
THAT SELF-LOVE CHIEFLY KEEPS A PERSON BACK FROM THE SOVEREIGN GOOD.

1. My Son, thou must give all for all, and be nothing of thy own.

Know that the love of thyself is more hurtful to thee than any thing in the world.

Every thing, according to the love and inclination which thou hast to it, cleaveth to thee more or less.

If thy love be pure, simple, and well ordered, thou shalt not be a captive to any thing.

Covet not that which thou mayest not have.

Seek not to have that which may hinder thee and rob thee of inward liberty.

It is wonderful that thou wilt not from the very bottom of thy heart commit thyself wholly to me, with all things that thou canst desire to have.

2. Why dost thou pine away with vain grief? why tirest thou thyself with useless cares?

Stand resigned to my good pleasure, and thou shalt suffer no loss.

If thou seekest this, or that, or wouldst be here or there, for the sake of thy own interest, or the pleasing thy own will, thou shall never be at rest, nor free from solicitude; for in every thing thou shalt find some defect, and in every place there will be some one that will cross thee.

8. It is not therefore the obtaining or multiplying things exteriorly that avails thee, but rather the despising of them, and cutting them up by the root out of thy heart; which I would not have thee to understand only with regard to money and riches, and also with regard to ambition and honour, and the desire of empty praise: all which things pass away with the world.

The place avails little, if the spirit of fervour be wanting; neither shall that peace stand long which is sought from abroad, if the state of thy heart want the true foundation, that is, if thou stand not in me: thou mayest change, but not better thyself.

For when occasion happens, thou shalt find that which thou didst fly from, and more.

A Prayer

For the cleansing of the Heart,
and the obtaining heavenly wisdom.

4. Confirm me, O God, by the grace of thy holy spirit. Give me power to be strengthened in the inward man, and to cast out of my heart all unprofitable care and trouble; let me not be drawn away with various desires of any thing whatsoever, whether it be of little or great value; but may I look upon all things as passing away, and upon my self as passing along with them.

For nothing is lasting under the sun, where all is vanity and affliction of spirit. O how wise is he who considers things in this manner!

5. Give me, O Lord, heavenly wisdom, that I may learn above all things to seek thee, and to find thee; above all things to relish thee, and to love thee, and to understand all other things, as they are, according to the order of thy wisdom.

Grant that I may prudently decline him that flatters me, and patiently bear with him that contradicts me.

For this is great wisdom, not to be moved with every wind of words, nor to give ear to the wicked flattering Siren; for thus shall we go on securely in the way we have begun.

CHAPTER XXVIII.
AGAINST THE TONGUES OF DETRACTORS.

1. Son, take it not to heart if some people think ill of thee, and say of thee what thou art not willing to hear.

Thou oughtest to think worse of thyself, and to believe that no one is weaker than thyself.

If thou walkest *interiorly*, thou wilt make small account of flying words.

It is no small prudence to be silent in the evil time, and to turn within to me, and not to be disturbed with the judgment of man.

2. Let not thy peace be in the tongues of men; for whether they put a good or bad construction on what thou doest, thou art still what thou art.

Where is true peace, and true glory? Is it not in me?

And he who covets not to please men, nor fears their displeasure, shall enjoy much peace.

All disquiet of heart, and distraction of our senses, arises from inordinate love, and vain fear.

CHAPTER XXIX.
HOW IN THE TIME OF TRIBULATION GOD IS TO BE INVOKED AND BLESSED.

1. Blessed, O Lord, be thy name for ever, who has been pleased that this trial and tribulation should come upon me.

I cannot fly from it, but must of necessity fly to thee; that thou mayest help me, and turn it to my good.

Lord I am now in tribulation, and my heart is not at ease; but I am much afflicted with my present suffering.

And now, dear father, what shall I say? I am taken, Lord, in these straits: O save me from this hour.

But for this reason I came into this hour, that thou mightest be glorified, when I shall be exceedingly humbled, and delivered by thee.

May it please thee, O Lord, to deliver me; for, poor wretch that I am! what can I do, and whither shall I go without thee?

Give me patience, O Lord, this time also.

Help me, O my God, and I will not fear how much soever I may be oppressed.

2. And now in the midst of these things, what shall I say? Lord, thy will be done: I have well deserved to be afflicted and troubled.

I must needs bear it; and would to God, it may be with patience, till the storm pass over, and it be better.

But thy Almighty hand is able to take away from me this temptation also, and to moderate its violence, lest I quite sink under it; as thou hast often done heretofore for me; *O my God, my mercy!*

And how much more difficult this is to me, so much easier to thee is *this change of the right hand of the Most High.* Psalms lxxvi.

CHAPTER XXX.
OF ASKING THE DIVINE ASSISTANCE, AND OF CONFIDENCE OF RECOVERING GRACE.

1. Son, I am the Lord, who give strength in the day of tribulation.

Come to me when it is not well with thee.

This is that which most of all hinders heavenly comfort, that thou art slow in turning thyself to prayer.

For before thou earnestly prayest to me, thou seekest in the mean time many comforts, and delightest thyself in outward things.

And hence it comes to pass, that all things avail thee little, till thou take notice that I am he who deliver those that trust in me: nor is there out of me any powerful help, nor profitable counsel, nor lasting remedy.

But now having recovered spirit after the storm, grow thou strong again in the light of my tender mercies; for I am at hand, saith the Lord, to repair all, not only to the full, but even with abundance, and above measure.

2. Is any thing difficult to me? Or shall I be like one that promises and does not perform?

Where is thy faith? Stand firmly, and with perseverance. Have patience, and be of good courage; comfort will come to thee in its proper season.

Wait for me, wait, I will come and cure thee.

It is a temptation that troubles thee, and a vain fear that frights thee.

What does the solicitude about future accidents bring thee but only sorrow upon sorrow? ***Sufficient for the day is the evil thereof.*** Matthew vi.

It is a vain and unprofitable thing, to conceive either grief or joy for future things, which perhaps will never happen.

3. But it is incident to man to be deluded with such vain imaginations; and a sign of a soul that is yet weak to be so easily drawn away by the suggestion of the enemy.

For he cares not whether it be with things true or false, that he abuses and deceives thee; whether he overthrows thee with the love of things present, or the fear of things to come.

Let not therefore thy heart be troubled, and let it not fear.

Believe in me, and trust in my mercy.

When thou thinkest I am far from thee, I am often nearest to thee.

When thou judgest that almost all is lost, then oftentimes it is that thou art in the way of the greatest gain of merit.

All is not lost, when any thing falls out otherwise than thou wouldst have it.

Thou must not judge according to the present feeling, nor give thyself up in such manner to any trouble from whencesoever it comes, nor take it so, as if all hope was gone of being delivered out of it.

4. Think not thyself wholly forsaken, although for a time I have sent thee some tribulation, or withdrawn from thee the comfort which thou desirest; for this is the way to the kingdom of heaven.

And without all doubt it is more expedient for thee, and for the rest of my servants, that you be exercised by adversities, than that you should have all things according to your inclination.

I know thy secret thoughts, I know that it is very expedient for thy soul that thou shouldest sometimes be left without gust, lest thou shouldst be puffed up with good success, and shouldst take a complaisance in thyself, imagining thyself to be what thou art not.

What I have given I can justly take away, and restore it again when I please.

5. When I give it, it is still mine; when I take it away again, I take not any thing that is thine; for *every good gift and every perfect gift is mine,* James i.

If I send thee affliction, or any adversity, repine not, neither let thy heart be cast down.

I can quickly raise thee up again, and turn all thy burden into joy.

Nevertheless, I am just, and greatly to be praised, when I deal thus with thee.

6. If thou thinkest rightly, and considerest things in truth, thou oughtest never to be so much dejected and troubled for any adversity;

But rather to rejoice and give thanks: yea, to account this a special subject of joy, that I do not spare thee, afflicting thee with sorrows.

As my Father hath loved me, I also have loved you, said I to my beloved disciples, (John xv.) whom certainly I did not send to temporal joys, but to great conflicts; not to honours, but to contempt; not to idleness, but to labours; not to rest, but to bring forth much fruit in patience. Remember these words, O my Son.

CHAPTER XXXI.
OF DISREGARDING ALL THINGS CREATED, THAT SO WE MAY FIND THE CREATOR.

1. Lord, I stand much in need of a grace yet greater, if I must arrive so far, that it may not be in the power of any man, nor any thing created, to hinder me;

For as long as any thing holds me, I cannot freely fly to thee.

He was desirous to fly freely to thee, who said, Who will give me wings like a dove, and I will fly and be at rest. Psalms liv.

[USCCB: Psalms lv. 7.]

What can be more at rest than a simple eye [that aims at nothing but God]?

And what can be more free, than he that desires nothing upon earth?

A man ought therefore to pass and ascend above every thing created, and perfectly to forsake himself, and in ecstasy of mind to stand and see that thou, the Maker of all things, hast no similitude with thy creatures.

And unless a man be at liberty from all things created, he cannot attend to things divine.

And this is the reason why there are found so few **contemplative** persons, because there are few that wholly sequester themselves from transitory and created things.

2. For this a great grace is required, which may elevate the soul, and carry her up above herself.

And unless a man be elevated in spirit, and set at liberty from all creatures, and wholly united to God; whatever he knows, and whatever he has, is of no great weight.

Long shall he be little, and lie grovelling beneath, who esteems any thing great but only the **one, immense, eternal Good.**

And whatsoever is not God is **nothing**, and ought to be accounted as **nothing**.

There is a great difference between the wisdom of an illuminated devout man, and the knowledge of a learned studious scholar.

Far more noble is that learning which flows from above, from the divine influence, than that which with labour is acquired by the wit of man.

3. Many are found to desire contemplation; but care not to practise those things which are required thereunto.

It is a great impediment that we stand in signs and sensible things, and have but little of perfect mortification.

I know not what it is, by what spirit we are led, or what we pretend to, who seem to be called **spiritual** persons; that we take so much pains, and have a greater solicitude for transitory and mean things; and scarce ever have our senses fully recollected to think of our own interior.

4. Alas! after a slight recollection, we presently get out of ourselves again; neither do we weigh well our works by a strict examination.

We take no notice where our affections lie; nor do we lament the great want of purity in all we do.

For all flesh had corrupted its way, and therefore the great flood ensued. **Genesis** vi. **and** vii.

As therefore our interior affection is much corrupted, it must needs be that the action which follows should be corrupted also; a testimony of the want of inward vigour.

From a pure heart proceeds the fruit of a good life.

5. We are apt to enquire how much a man has done; but with how much virtue he has done it, is not so diligently considered.

We ask whether he be strong, rich, beautiful, ingenious, a good writer, a good singer, or a good workman; but how poor he is in spirit, how patient and meek, how devout and internal, is what few speak of.

Nature looks upon the outward thing of a man, but grace turns herself to the interior.

Nature is often deceived, but grace hath her trust in God, that she may not be deceived.

CHAPTER XXXII.
OF THE DENYING OURSELVES, AND RENOUNCING ALL CUPIDITY.

1. Son, thou canst not possess perfect liberty, unless thou wholly deny thyself.

All self-seekers and self-lovers are bound in fetters, full of desires, full of cares, unsettled, and seeking always their own ease, and not the things of Jesus Christ, but oftentimes devising and framing that which shall not stand;

For all shall come to nothing that proceeds not from God.

Take this short and perfect word, Forsake all and thou shall find all, leave thy desires and thou shall find rest.

Consider this well, and when thou shalt put it in practice thou shalt understand all things.

2. Lord, this is not the work of one day, nor children's sport; yea, in this short sentence is included the whole perfection of the religious.

Son, thou must not be turned back, nor presently cast down, when thou hearest what the way of the perfect is, but rather be incited thereby to undertake great things, or at least to sigh after them with an earnest desire.

I would it were so with thee, and that thou wert come so far that thou wert no longer a lover of thyself, but didst stand wholly at my beck, and at his whom I have appointed father over thee; then wouldst thou exceedingly please me, and all thy life would pass in joy and peace.

Thou hast yet many things to forsake, which unless thou give up to me without reserve, thou shalt not attain to that which thou demandest.

I counsel thee to buy of me gold tried in the fire, that thou mayest become rich. Apoc. iii.

That is heavenly wisdom, which treads under foot all things below.

Set aside the wisdom of the earth, *i.e.* seeking to please the world and thyself.

3. I have said that thou shouldst give the things that are high and of great esteem with men, to purchase those which are esteemed contemptible;

For true heavenly wisdom seems very mean and contemptible, and is scarce thought of by men; that wisdom which teaches to think meanly of one's self, and not to seek to become great upon earth, which many praise; in words, but in their life they are far from it; yet this same is that *precious, pearl*, which is hidden from many. *Matthew* xiii.

CHAPTER XXXIII.
OF THE INCONSTANCY OF OUR HEART, AND OF DIRECTING OUR FINAL INTENTION TO GOD.

1. Son, trust not to thy present affection, it will quickly be changed into another.

As long as thou livest thou art subject to change, even against thy will; so as to be sometimes joyful, other times sad; now easy, anon troubled; at one time devout, at another dry; sometimes fervent, other times sluggish; one day heavy, another lighter.

But he that is wise and well instructed in *spirit* stands above all these changes; not minding what he feels in himself, nor on what side the wind of mutability blows; but that the whole bent of his soul may advance towards its due and wished-for end;

For so he may continue one and the self-same without being shaken, by directing without ceasing, through all this variety of events, the single eye of his intention towards me.

2. And by how much the purer the eye of the intention is, by so much the more constantly may one pass these diverse storms.

But in many the eye of pure intention is dark, for we quickly look towards something delightful which comes in our way;

And it is rare to find one wholly free from all blemish of self-seeking.

So the Jews heretofore came into Bethania to Martha and Mary, not for Jesus only, but that they might see Lazarus also. *John* xi.

The eye of the intention therefore must be purified, that it may be single and right; and must be directed unto me, beyond all the various objects that interpose themselves.

CHAPTER XXXIV.
THAT HE THAT LOVES GOD RELISHES HIM ABOVE ALL THINGS, AND IN ALL THINGS.

1. Behold *my* God, *and my All*, What would I have more, and what can I desire more happy?

O savoury and sweet word! but to him that loves *the Word*, not the world, nor the things that are in the world.

My God, *and All!* Enough is said to him that understands; and it is delightful to him that loves to repeat it often.

For when thou art present all things yield delight; but when thou art absent, all things are loathsome.

Thou givest tranquillity to the heart, and great peace, and pleasant joy.

Thou makest to think well of all, and praise thee in all things; nor can any thing without thee afford any lasting pleasure: but to make it agreeable and relishing, thy grace must be present; and it must be seasoned with the seasoning of thy wisdom.

2. He that has a relish of thee will find all things savoury.

And to him that relishes thee not, what can ever yield any true delight?

But the wise of this world, and the admirers of the flesh, are far from the relish of thy wisdom; because in the world is much vanity, and the following of the flesh leads to death.

But they that follow thee, by despising the things of this world, and mortifying the flesh, are found to be wise indeed: for they are translated from vanity to truth, from the flesh to the spirit.

Such as these have a relish of God; and what good soever is found in creatures, they refer it all to the praise of their Maker.

But great, yea very great, is the difference between the relish of the Creator and the creature; of eternity and of time; of light increated, and of light enlightened.

3. O Light eternal, transcending all created lights, dart forth thy lightning from above, which may penetrate all the most inward parts of my heart.

Cleanse, cherish, enlighten, and enliven my spirit with its powers, that it may be absorpt in thee with ecstasies of joy.

Oh! when will this blessed and desirable hour come, that thou shalt fill me with thy presence, and become to me *All in All?*

As long as this is not granted me, my joy will not be full.

Alas! the old man is still living in me; he is not wholly crucified; he is not perfectly dead:

He still lusts strongly against the spirit; he wages war within me, and suffers not the kingdom of my soul to be quiet.

4. But, O Lord, who rulest over the power of the sea, and assuagest the motion of its waves, (Psalms lxxxviii.) arise and help me.

[USCCB: Psalms lxxxix. 10.]

Dissipate the people that desire war. Psalms lxvii. Crush them by thy power.

Shew forth, I beseech thee, thy wonderful works; and let thy right-hand be glorified: for there is no other help nor refuge for me, but in thee, O Lord, my God.

CHAPTER XXXV.
THAT THERE IS NO BEING SECURE FROM TEMPTATION IN THIS LIFE.

1. Son, thou art never secure in this life; but as long as thou livest thou hast always need of spiritual arms.

Thou art in the midst of enemies, and art assaulted on all sides.

If then thou dost not make use of the buckler of patience, thou wilt not be long without wounds.

Moreover, if thou dost not fix thy heart on me, with a sincere will of suffering all things for my sake, thou canst not support the heat of this warfare, nor attain to the victory of the saints. It behoveth thee therefore to go through all manfully, and to use a strong hand against all things that oppose thee.

For *to him that overcomes is given manna*, (Apoc. ii.) and to the sluggard is left much misery.

2. If thou seekest rest in this life, how then wilt thou come to rest everlasting?

Set not thy self to seek for much rest, but for much patience.

Seek true peace, not upon earth, but in heaven; not in men, nor in other things created, but in God alone.

Thou must be willing, for the love of God, to suffer all things, *viz.* labours and sorrows, temptations and vexations, anxieties, necessities, sicknesses, injuries, detractions, reprehensions, humiliations, confusions, corrections, and contempts.

These things help to obtain virtue: these try a novice of Christ: these procure a heavenly crown.

I will give an everlasting reward for this short labour, and glory without end for transitory confusion.

3. Dost thou think to have always spiritual consolations when thou pleasest?

My saints had not so; but met with many troubles, and various temptations and great desolations.

But they bore all with patience, and confided more in God than in themselves; knowing that the sufferings of this life are not of equal proportion to the merit of the glory to come.

Wouldst thou have that immediately, which others after many tears and great labours have hardly obtained?

Expect the Lord, do manfully, and be of good heart. Do not despond, do not fall off; but constantly offer both soul and body for the glory of God.

I will reward thee most abundantly, and will be with thee in all thy tribulations.

CHAPTER XXXVI.
AGAINST THE VAIN JUDGMENTS OF MEN.

1. Son, cast thy heart firmly on the Lord, and fear not the judgement of man, when thy conscience gives testimony of thy piety and innocence.

It is good and happy to suffer in this manner, neither will this be grievous to an humble heart, nor to him that trusts in God more than in himself.

Many say many things, and therefore little credit is to be given to them.

Neither is it possible to satisfy all;

Though Paul endeavoured to please all in the Lord, and made himself all unto all: yet at the same time he made little account of his being judged by man's day. 1 *Corinthians* iv. *and* ix.

2. He labours for the edification and salvation of others, as much as he could, and as lay in him; but he could not prevent his being sometimes judged or despised by others.

Therefore he committed all to God, who knows all; and defended himself by patience and humility against the tongues of those that spoke evil, or thought and gave out at pleasure vain and faulty things of him.

However, he answered them sometimes, lest his silence might give occasion of scandal to the weak.

3. Who art thou, that thou shouldst be afraid of a mortal man? To-day he is, and to-morrow he appears no more.

Fear God, and thou shalt have no need of being afraid of man.

What can any one do against thee, by his words or injuries? He rather hurts himself than thee; nor can he escape the judgment of God whoever he be.

See thou have God before thine eyes; and do not contend with complaining words.

And if at present thou seem to be overcome, and to suffer a confusion which thou hast not deserved; do not repine at this, and do not lessen thy crown by impatience.

But rather look up to me in heaven, who am able to deliver thee from all confusion and wrong, and to repay every one according to his works.

CHAPTER XXXVII.
OF A PURE AND FULL RESIGNATION OF OURSELVES, FOR THE OBTAINING FREEDOM OF HEART.

1. Son, leave thyself, and thou shalt find me.

Stand without choice, or any self-seeking; and thou shalt always gain.

For the greater grace shall always be added to thee, when thou hast perfectly given up thyself, without resuming thyself again.

2. Lord, how often shall I resign myself; and in what things shall I leave myself?

3. Always, and at all times; as in little, so also in great: I make no exception, but will have thee to be found in all things stript of thyself.

Otherwise how canst thou be mine, and I thine; unless thou be both within and without freed from all self-will?

The sooner thou effectest this, the better will it be for thee; and the more fully and sincerely thou dost it, the more shalt thou please me, and the more shalt thou gain.

4. Some there are that resign themselves, but it is with some exception; for they do not trust wholly to God, and therefore are busy to provide for themselves. Some also at the first offer all; but afterwards, being assaulted by temptation, return again to what they left; and therefore they make no progress in virtue.

These shall not attain to the true liberty of a pure heart, nor to the grace of a delightful familiarity with me; unless they first entirely resign themselves up, and offer themselves a daily sacrifice to me; for without this, divine union neither is nor will be obtained.

5. I have often said to thee, and I repeat it now again, forsake thyself, resign thyself, and thou shalt enjoy a great inward peace.

Give all for all, seek nothing, call for nothing back, stand purely, and with a full confidence in me, and thou shalt have me.

Thou shalt be at liberty within thy own heart, and darkness shall not overwhelm thee.

Aim only at this, pray for this, desire this, that thou mayest be stript of self-seeking, and thus naked follow thy naked Jesus; that thou mayest die to thyself, and live eternally to me.

Then all vain imaginations shall vanish, all evil disturbances, and superfluous cares.

Then also immoderate fear shall leave thee, and inordinate love shall die.

CHAPTER XXXVIII.
OF THE GOOD GOVERNMENT OF OURSELVES IN OUTWARD THINGS, AND OF HAVING RECOURSE TO GOD IN DANGERS.

1. Son, thou must diligently make it thy aim, that in every place, and in every action or outward employment, thou be inwardly free, and master of thyself; and that all things be under thee, and not thou under them.

That thou mayest be lord and ruler of thy actions, and not a slave or bondsman:

But rather a freeman, and a true Hebrew transferred to the lot and to the liberty of the children of God;

Who stand above the things present, and contemplate those that are eternal; who look upon transitory things with the left eye, and with the right the things of heaven.

Who suffer not themselves to be drawn away by temporal things to cleave to them; but they rather draw these things to themselves, to make them serviceable to that end, for which they were ordained by God, and appointed by that Sovereign Artist, who has left nothing in all his works but regular and orderly.

2. If likewise, in all events, thou rulest not thyself by the outward appearance; nor lookest on the things which thou seest or hearest, with a carnal eye; but presently, on every occasion, doth enter like Moses into the tabernacle to consult the Lord; thou shalt sometimes hear the divine answer, and come out instructed in many things present and to come.

For Moses always had recourse to the tabernacle, for the deciding all doubts and questions; and fled to the help of prayer, against the dangers and wickedness of men:

So must thou in like manner fly to the closet of thy heart, and there most earnestly implore the divine assistance: for Joshua and the children of Israel, as we read, (*Joshua* ix.) were therefore deceived by the Gabaonites; because they did not first consult the Lord, but too easily giving credit to fair words, were deluded with counterfeit piety.

CHAPTER XXXIX.
THAT A MAN MUST NOT BE OVER EAGER IN HIS AFFAIRS.

1. Son, always commit thy cause to me; I will dispose well of it in due season. Wait for my disposal, and thou shalt find it will be for thy advantage.

2. Lord, I willingly commit all things to thee; for my care can profit little.

I wish I was not too much set upon future events; but offered myself with all readiness to thy divine pleasure.

3. My Son, oftentimes a man eagerly sets about a thing which he desires; but when he has obtained it, he begins to be of another mind: for our inclinations are not wont to continue long upon the same thing, but rather pass from one thing to another.

It is therefore a thing not of the least importance, to forsake one's self even in the least things.

4. A man's true progress consists in denying himself; and the man that has renounced himself is very much at liberty, and very safe.

But the old enemy, who opposes all that is good, fails not to tempt; but day and night lays his dangerous plots to withdraw the unwary into his deceitful snare. **Watch and pray**, saith the Lord, ***that ye enter not into temptation***. Matthew xxvi.

CHAPTER XL.
THAT MAN HATH NO GOOD OF HIMSELF, AND THAT HE CANNOT GLORY IN ANY THING.

3. Lord, what is man that thou art mindful of him; or the Son of Man that thou vouchsafest to visit him? Psalms vi.

What hath man deserved, that thou shouldst give him thy grace?

Lord what cause have I to complain if thou forsake me? Or what can I justly alledge, if thou refuse to grant my petition?

This, indeed, I may truly think and say: Lord, *I am nothing, I can do nothing, I have nothing of myself that is good;* but I fail and am defective in all things, and ever tend to *nothing;*

And unless I am supported and interiorly instructed by thee, I become quite tepid and dissolute.

2. But thou, O Lord, art always the same, and endureth for ever; always good, just and holy; doing all things well, justly, and holily; and disposing them in wisdom.

But I, who am more inclined to go back than to go forward, continue not always in one state; for seven different seasons are changed over me.

Yet it quickly becomes better when it pleaseth thee, and thou stretchest out thy helping hand: for thou alone, without man's aid, canst assist me, and so strengthen me, that my countenance shall be no more changed, but my heart shall be converted, and take its rest in thee alone.

3. Wherefore if I did but well know how to cast away from me all human comfort, either for the sake of devotion, or through the necessity of seeking thee, because there is no man that can comfort me.

Then might I justly depend on thy grace, and rejoice in the gift of new consolation.

4. Thanks be to thee, from whom all proceeds as often as it goes well with me.

But, for my part, I am but mere vanity, and nothing in thy sight; an unconstant and weak man.

What have I then to glory in? or why do I desire to be esteemed?

Is it not for nothing? And this is most vain.

Truly, vain-glory is an evil plague, a very great vanity; because it draws us away from true glory, and robs us of heavenly grace.

For whilst a man takes a complacence in himself, he displeaseth thee; whilst he gapes after the praises of men, he is deprived of true virtues.

5. But true glory and holy joy is to glory in thee, and not in one's self; to rejoice in thy name, and not to be delighted in one's own virtue, nor in any creature, save only for thy sake.

Let thy name be praised, not mine: let thy work be extolled, not mine: let thy holy name be blessed, but to me let nothing be attributed of the praises of men.

Thou art my glory, thou art the joy of my heart:

In thee will I glory and rejoice all the day; but for myself I will glory in nothing but in my infirmities.

6. Let the Jews seek the glory which one man receives from another: I will seek that which is from God alone.

All human glory, all temporal honour, all worldly grandeur, compared to thy eternal glory, is but vanity and foolishness.

O my truth, and my mercy, my God, O blessed Trinity, to thee alone be all praise, honour, power, and glory, for endless ages of ages.

CHAPTER XLI.
OF THE CONTEMPT OF ALL TEMPORAL HONOUR.

1. My Son, take it not to heart, if thou seest others honoured and advanced, and thyself despised and debased.

Lift up thy heart to me in heaven, and thou wilt not be concerned at thy being contemned by men upon earth.

2. Lord, we are in blindness, and are quickly seduced by vanity. If I look well into myself, never was any injury done me by any creature; and therefore I cannot justly complain of thee.

For, because I have often and grievously sinned against thee, all creatures have reason to take up arms against me.

To me therefore confusion and contempt is justly due, but to thee praise, honour, and glory.

And unless I put myself in this disposition, to be willing to be despised and forsaken of all creatures, and to be esteemed nothing at all, I cannot arrive at inward peace and strength, nor be spiritually enlightened, nor fully united to thee.

CHAPTER XLII.
THAT OUR PEACE IS NOT TO BE PLACED IN MEN.

1. Son, if thou placest thy peace with any person, for the sake of thy contentment in his company, thou shall be unsettled and entangled:

But if thou hast recourse to the everliving and subsisting Truth, thou shalt not be grieved when a friend departs or dies.

In *me* the love of thy friend must stand; and for *me* is he to be loved, whoever he be, who appears to thee good, and is very dear to thee in this life.

Without *me* no friendship is of any strength, nor will be durable; nor is that love true and pure of which I am not the author.

Thou oughtest to be so far mortified to such affections of persons beloved, as to wish (for as much as appertains to thee) to be without any company of man.

By so much the more does a man draw nigh to God, by how much the farther he withdraws himself from all earthly comfort.

So much the higher he ascends into God, by how much the lower he descends into himself, and by how much the meaner he esteems himself.

2. But he that attributes any thing of good to himself, stops the grace of God from coming into him; for the grace of the Holy Ghost ever seeks an humble heart.

If thou couldst perfectly annihilate thyself, and cast out from thyself all created love, then should I flow into thee with abundance of grace.

When thou lookest towards creatures, the sight of the Creator is withdrawn from thee.

Learn for the Creator's sake, to overcome thyself in all things; and then thou shalt be able to attain to the knowledge of God.

How little soever it be, if a thing be inordinately loved and regarded, it keeps us back from the Sovereign Good, and corrupts the soul.

CHAPTER XLIII.
AGAINST VAIN AND WORLDLY LEARNING.

1. Son, be not moved with the fine and quaint sayings of men: *For the kingdom of God consists not in talk, but in virtue*.

Attend to my words, which inflame the heart, and enlighten the mind: which excite to compunction, and afford manifold consolations.

Never read any thing that thou may appear more learned or more wise.

Study therefore to mortify thy vices, for this will avail thee more than the knowledge of many hard questions.

2. When thou shalt have read, and shalt know many things, thou must always return to one beginning.

I am he that teacheth man knowledge, and I give a more clear understanding to little ones than can be taught by man.

He to whom I speak will quickly be wise, and will make great progress in spirit.

Wo to them that enquire of men after many curious things, and are little curious of the way to serve me.

The time will come, when Christ, the Master of masters, the Lord of angels, shall appeal, to hear the lessons of all men; that is, to examine the consciences of every one.

And then he will search Jerusalem with candles, and the hidden things of darkness shall be brought to light, and the arguments of tongues shall be silent.

3. I am he that in an instant elevates an humble mind, to comprehend more reasons of the *eternal truth* than could be got by ten years study in the schools.

I teach without noise of words, without confusion of opinions, without ambition of honour, without contention of arguments.

I teach to despise all earthly things, to loathe things present, to seek things eternal, to relish things eternal, to fly honours, to endure scandals, to repose all hope in me, to desire nothing out of me, and above all things ardently to love me.

4. For a certain person, by loving me, entirely learned divine things, and spoke wonders.

He profited more by forsaking all things, than by studying subtleties.

But to some I speak things common, to others things more particular; to some I sweetly appear in signs and figures; to others in great light I reveal mysteries.

The voice of the books is the same, but it teacheth not all men alike; because I within am the teacher of truth, the searcher of hearts, the understander of thoughts, the promoter of actions; distributing to every one as I judge fitting.

CHAPTER XLIV.
OF NOT DRAWING TO OURSELVES EXTERIOR THINGS.

1. Son, in many things it behoveth thee to be ignorant and to esteem thyself as one dead upon earth, and as one to whom the whole world is crucified.

Many things also must you pass by with a deaf ear, and think rather of those things that appertain to thy peace.

It is more profitable to turn away thy eyes from such things as displease thee, and to leave to every one his own way of thinking, than to give way to contentious discourses.

If thou standeth well with God, and lookest at his judgment, thou wilt more easily bear to see thyself overcome.

2. O Lord, to what are we come? Behold a temporal loss is greatly bewailed, for a small gain men labour and toil; but the loss of the soul is little thought on, and hardly ever returns to mind.

That which is of little or no profit takes up our thoughts; and that which is above all things necessary is negligently passed over: for the whole man sinks down into outward things; and unless he quickly recovers himself, he willingly continues immersed in them.

CHAPTER XLV.
THAT CREDIT IS NOT TO BE GIVEN TO ALL MEN; AND THAT MEN ARE PRONE TO OFFEND IN WORDS.

1. Grant me help, O Lord, in my tribulation, for vain is the aid of man. Psalms lix.

[USCCB: Psalms lx. 13.]

How often have I not found faith there, where I thought I might depend upon it?

And how often have I found it where I did not expect it?

Vain therefore is all hope in men; but the safety of the Just is in thee, O Lord.

Blessed be thou, O Lord my God, in all things that befal us.

We are weak and unsettled, we are quickly deceived and changed.

2. Who is the man that is able to keep himself so warily, and with so much circumspection in all things, as not to fall sometimes into some deceit or perplexity?

But he that trusts in thee, O Lord, and seeks thee with a simple heart, does not so easily fall;

And if he lights into some tribulation, in what manner soever he may be entangled therewith, he will quickly be rescued or comforted by thee; for thou wilt not forsake forever him that trusts in thee.

A trusty friend is rarely to be found, that continues faithful in all the distresses of his friend.

Thou, O Lord, thou alone art most faithful in all things, and besides thee there is no other such.

3. Oh! how wise was that holy soul that said, **My mind is strongly settled and grounded upon Christ**. St. Agatha.

If it were so with me, the fear of man would not so easily give me trouble, nor flying words move me.

Who can foresee all things, or who is able to provide against all future evils?

If things foreseen do yet often hurt us, how can things unlooked for fail of wounding us grievously?

But why did I not provide better for myself, miserable wretch as I am? Why also have I so easily given credit to others?

But we are men, and are but frail men, though by many we are reputed and called angels.

To whom shall I give credit, O Lord? to whom but thee? Thou art the truth, which neither canst deceive nor be deceived.

And on the other side, **Every man is a liar**, (Psalms cxi.) infirm, unstable, and subject to fail, especially in words; so that we ought not readily to believe even that which in appearance seems to sound well.

4. How wisely didst thou forewarn us to take heed of men, (**Matthew**. x. 17.) and that man's enemies are those of his own household. (**Matthew**. x. 36.) And that we are not to believe, if any one should say, **Behold here, or behold there**. Matthew xxiv.

I have been taught to my cost, and I wish it may serve to make me more cautious, and not to increase my folly.

Be wary, saith one, be wary, keep in thyself what I tell thee: and whilst I hold my peace, and believe the matter to be secret, he himself cannot keep the secret which he desired me to keep, but presently discovers both me and himself, and goes his way.

From such tales and such unwary people defend me, O Lord, that I may not fall into their hands, nor ever commit the like.

Give to my mouth truth and constancy in my words, and remove far from me a crafty tongue.

What I am not willing to suffer, I ought by all means to shun.

5. O how good a thing and how peaceable it is to be silent of others, nor to believe all that is said, nor easily to report what one has heard; to lay one's self open to few; always to seek thee the Beholder of the Heart; and not to be carried about with every wind of words; but to wish that all things both within and without us may go according to the pleasure of thy will!

How secure it is for the keeping of heavenly grace, to fly the sight of men, and not to seek those things that seem to cause admiration abroad; but with all diligence to follow that which brings amendment of life and fervour!

To how many hath it been hurtful to have their virtue known, and over-hastily praised? How profitable indeed hath grace been kept with silence in this frail life, which is all but a temptation and a warfare?

CHAPTER XLVI.
OF HAVING CONFIDENCE IN GOD, WHEN WORDS ARISE AGAINST US.

1. Son, stand firm, and trust in me; for what are words but words? they fly through the air, but hurt not a stone.

If thou art guilty, think that thou wilt willingly amend thyself.

If thy conscience accuse thee not, think that thou wilt willingly suffer this for God's sake.

It is a small matter that thou shouldst sometimes bear with words, if thou hast not as yet the courage to endure hard stripes.

And why do such small things go to thy heart; but because thou art yet carnal, and regardest man more than thou oughtest?

For because thou art afraid of being despised, thou art not willing to be reprehended for thy faults, and seekest to shelter thyself in excuses.

2. But look better into thyself, and thou shalt find that the world is still living in thee, and a vain desire of pleasing men:

For when thou art unwilling to be humbled and confounded for thy defects, it is plain indeed that thou art not truly humble, nor truly dead to the world, nor the world crucified to thee.

But give ear to my word, and thou shalt not value ten thousand words of men.

Behold, if all should be said against thee, which the malice of men can invent, what hurt could it do thee, if thou wouldst let it pass, and make no reckoning of it? Could it even so much as pluck one hair away from thee?

3. But he who has not his heart *within*, nor God before his eyes, is easily moved with a word of dispraise:

Whereas he that trusts in me, and desires not to stand by his own judgment, will be free from the fear of men.

For I am the judge and discerner of all secrets; I know how the matter passed; I know both him that offers the injury, and him that suffers it.

From me this word went forth; by my permission it happened, *that out of many hearts thoughts may be revealed*. Luke ii.

I shall judge the guilty and the innocent; but by a secret judgment I would beforehand try them both.

4. The testimony of men oftentimes deceives: my judgment is true, it shall stand and not be overthrown.

It is hidden for the most part, and to few laid open in every thing; yet it never errs, nor can it err, though to the eyes of fools it seems not right.

To me therefore must thou run in every judgment, and not depend upon thy own will.

For the just man will not be troubled whatever happens to him from God. Proverbs xii.

And if any thing be wrongfully pronounced against him, he will not much care; neither will he vainly rejoice, if by others he be reasonably excused; for he considers that *I am he that searcheth the heart and the reins*, (Apoc. ii.) who judge not according to the face, nor according to human appearance;

[USCCB: Revelation 3:23, "...I am the
*searcher of hearts and **minds**...".]*

For oftentimes that is found blameworthy in my eyes, which in the judgment of men is esteemed commendable.

5. O Lord God, the best judge, strong and patient, who knowest the frailty and perverseness of men, be thou my strength, and all my confidence, for my own conscience sufficeth me not.

Thou knowest that which I know not; and therefore in every reprehension I ought to humble myself, and bear it with meekness.

Pardon me, I beseech thee in thy mercy, as often as I have not done thus, and give me again the grace to suffer still more.

For better to me is thy great mercy, for the obtaining of pardon, than the justice which I imagine in myself for the defence of my hidden conscience.

Although my conscience accuse me not, yet I cannot hereby justify myself; for setting thy mercy aside, **no man living shall be justified in thy sight**. Psalms cxlii.

[USCCB: Psalms cxliii.]

CHAPTER XLVII.
THAT ALL GRIEVIOUS THINGS ARE TO BE ENDURED FOR LIFE EVERLASTING.

1. Son, be not dismayed with the labours which thou hast undertaken for me; neither let the tribulations which befal thee quite cast thee down; but let my promise strengthen thee, and comfort thee in all events.

I am sufficient to reward thee beyond all measure.

Thou shalt not labour here long, nor shalt thou be always oppressed with sorrows.

Wait a little while, and thou shalt see a speedy end of all thy evils.

The hour will come when labour and trouble shall be no more.

All is little and short which passeth away with time.

2. Mind what thou art about; labour faithfully in my vineyard; I will be thy reward.

Write, read, sing, sigh, keep silence, pray, bear thy crosses manfully: eternal life is worthy of all these, and greater combats.

Peace shall come in one day, which is known to the Lord: and it shall not be day, nor night, *viz.* such as is at present, but everlasting light, infinite brightness, steadfast peace, and secure rest.

Thou shalt not then say, ***Who shall deliver me from the body of this death***, (Romans vii.) nor shalt thou cry out, ***Wo to me for that my sojourning is prolonged***. (Psalms cxix.) For death shall be no more; but never failing health, no anxiety, but blessed delight, and a society sweet and lovely.

[USCCB: Psalms cxx. 6. "Too long did I live
among those who hated peace."]

3. Oh! if thou hadst seen the everlasting crowns of the saints in heaven, and in how great glory they now triumph, who appeared contemptible heretofore to this world, and in a manner unworthy even of life, doubtless thou wouldst immediately cast thyself down to the very earth, and wouldst rather seek to be under the feet of all, than to have command so much as over one.

Neither wouldst thou covet the pleasant days of this life, but wouldst rather be glad to suffer tribulation for God's sake, and esteem it thy greatest gain to be reputed as nothing amongst men.

4. Ah! if thou didst but relish these things, and didst suffer them to penetrate deeply thy heart, how wouldst thou dare so much as once to complain!

Are not all painful labours to be endured for everlasting life?

It is no small matter to lose or to gain the kingdom of God.

Lift up therefore thy face to heaven. Behold I, and all my saints with me, who in this world have had a great conflict, do now rejoice, are comforted now, are now secure, are now at rest, and for all eternity shall abide with me in the kingdom of my Father.

CHAPTER XLVIII.
OF THE DAY OF ETERNITY, AND OF THE MISERIES OF THIS LIFE.

1. O Most happy mansion of the city above! O most bright day of eternity, which knows no night, but is always enlightened by the Sovereign Truth; a day always joyful, always secure, and never changing its state for the contrary!

Oh! that this day would shine upon us, and all these temporal things would come to an end!

It shines indeed upon the saints, resplendant with everlasting brightness; but to us pilgrims upon earth it is seen only as afar off, and through a glass.

2. The citizens of heaven know how joyful that day is; but the banished children of Eve lament that this our day is bitter and tedious.

The days of this life are short and evil, full of sorrows and miseries: where man is defiled with many sins, is ensnared with many passions, attacked with many fears, disquieted with many cares, distracted with many curiosities, entangled with many vanities, encompassed with many errors, broken with many labours, troubled with temptations, weakened with delights, tormented with want.

3. Oh! when will there be an end of these evils? When shall I be set at liberty from the wretched slavery of sin?

When, O Lord, shall I be so happy as to think of thee alone? When shall I to the full rejoice in thee?

When shall I be without any impediment in true liberty, without any trouble of mind or body?

When shall I enjoy a solid peace, a peace never to be disturbed and always secure, a peace both within and without, a peace every where firm?

O good Jesu, when shall I stand to behold thee?

When shall I contemplate the glory of thy kingdom? When wilt thou be *all in all* to me? O when shall I be with thee in thy kingdom, which thou hast prepared for thy Beloved from all eternity?

I am left a poor and banished man, in an enemy's country, where there are wars every day, and very great misfortunes.

4. Comfort me in my banishment, assuage my sorrows; for all my desire is after thee: and all that this world offers for my comfort is burthensome to me.

I long to enjoy thee intimately, but cannot attain to it.

I desire to cleave to heavenly things, but the things of this life and my unmortified passions bear me down. I am willing in *mind* to be above all things, but by the flesh am obliged against my will to be subject to them.

Thus, unhappy man that I am, I fight with myself, and am become burthensome to myself, whilst the spirit seeks to tend upwards, and the flesh downwards.

5. Oh! what do I suffer interiorly, whilst in my mind I consider heavenly things, and presently a crowd of carnal thoughts offers to interrupt my prayer? *O my God, remove not thyself far from me, and depart not in thy wrath from thy servant.*

Dart forth thy lightning, and disperse them: shoot thy arrows, and let all the phantoms of the enemy be put to flight.

Gather my senses together to thee; make me forget all worldly things; give me the grace speedily to cast away and to despise all wicked imaginations.

Come to my aid, O eternal *truth*, that no vanity may move me.

Come, heavenly sweetness, and let all impurity fly before thy face.

Pardon me also, and mercifully forgive me the times that I have thought of any thing else in prayer besides thee.

For I confess truly, that I am accustomed to be very much distracted:

For oftentimes I am not there, where I am bodily standing or sitting, but am rather there where my thoughts carry me.

There I am, where my thought is: and there oftentimes is my thought, where that is which I love.

That thing most readily comes to my mind, which naturally delights me, or which through custom is pleasing to me.

6. For this reason thou, who art the *truth*, hast plainly said, **Where thy treasure is, there also is thy heart**. Matthew vi.

If I love heaven, I willingly think of heavenly things.

If I love the world, I rejoice in the prosperity of the world, and am troubled at its adversity.

If I love the flesh, my imagination is often taken up with the things of the flesh.

If I love the spirit, I delight to think of spiritual things.

For whatsoever things I love, of the same I willingly speak and hear, and carry home with me the images of them.

But blessed is the man, who for thee, O Lord, lets go all things created: who offers violence to his nature; and through fervour of spirit crucifies the lusts of the flesh: that so his conscience being cleared up, he may offer to thee *pure* prayer, and may be worthy to be admitted, among the choirs of angels, having shut out all things of the earth both from without and within.

CHAPTER XLIX.
OF THE DESIRE OF ETERNAL LIFE: AND HOW GREAT THINGS ARE PROMISED TO THEM THAT FIGHT.

1. Son, when thou perceivest a longing after eternal bliss to be infused into thee from above, and that thou desirest to go out of the dwelling of this body, that thou mayest contemplate my brightness, without any shadow of change; dilate thy heart, and with all thy affection embrace this holy inspiration.

Return very great thanks to the divine bounty, which deals so favourably with thee, which mercifully delivers thee, ardently excites thee, and powerfully raises thee up, lest by thy own weight thou fall down to the things of the earth.

For it is not by thy own thought or endeavours that thou attainest to this; but only by the favour of heavenly grace and the divine visit: that so thou mayest advance in virtues, and greater humility, and prepare thyself for future conflicts, and labour with the whole affection of thy heart to stick close to me, and serve me with a fervent will.

2. Son, the fire often burns, but the flame ascends not without smoke:

So also some people's desires are on fire after heavenly things, and yet they are not free from temptation of fleshly affection:

And therefore it is not altogether purely for God's honour that they do what they so earnestly request of him.

Such also is oftentimes thy desire, which thou hast signified to be so strong.

For that is not pure and perfect, which is infected with self-interest.

4. Ask not what is delightful and commodious for thee, but what is pleasing and honourable to me: for if thou judgest rightly, thou oughtest to follow my appointment rather than thy own desire, and to prefer it before all that thou desirest.

I know thy desire, and I have often heard thy sighs.

Thou wouldst be glad to be at present in the liberty of the glory of the children of God:

Thou wouldst be pleased to be now at thy eternal home, and in thy heavenly country abounding with joy: but that hour is not yet come; for there is yet another time, *viz*. a time of war, a time of labour and trial.

Thou wishest to be replenished with the Sovereign Good, but thou canst not at present attain to it.

I am [that Sovereign Good] wait for me, saith the Lord, till the kingdom of God comes.

4. Thou must yet be tried upon earth, and exercised in many things.

Consolation shall sometimes be given thee; but to be fully satisfied shall not be granted thee.

Take courage therefore, and be valiant as well in doing as in suffering things repugnant to nature.

Thou must put on the new man, and be changed into another man.

Thou must oftentimes do that which is against thy inclination, and let alone that which thou art inclined to:

That which is pleasing to others shall go forward, that which thou wouldst have shall not succeed:

That which others say, shall be hearkened to; what thou sayest shall not be regarded:

Others shall ask, and shall receive; thou shalt ask, and not obtain.

5. Others shall be great in the esteem of men; but of thee no notice shall be taken.

To others this or that shall be committed; but thou shalt be accounted fit for nothing.

At this nature will sometimes repine, and it will be no small matter if thou bear it with silence.

In these and many such like things, the faithful servant of the Lord is used to be tried, how far he can renounce himself, and break himself in all things.

There is scarce any one thing in which thou standest so much in need of mortifying thyself, as in seeing and suffering the things that are repugnant to thy will; and especially when that is commanded which seems to thee incongruous and to little purpose.

And because being under authority thou darest not resist the higher power, therefore thou art apt to think it hard to walk at the beck of another, and wholly to give up thy own sentiment.

6. But consider, Son, the fruit of these labours, how quickly they will end, and their exceeding great reward; and thou wilt not be troubled at them, but strongly comforted in thy sufferings.

For in regard of the little of thy will, which thou now willingly forsakest, thou shalt for ever have thy will in heaven.

For there thou shalt find all that thou willest, all that thou canst desire.

There thou shalt enjoy all good without fear of ever losing it.

There thy will being always one with mine, shall desire nothing foreign or private.

There no one shall resist thee, no man shall complain of thee, no man shall hinder thee, nothing shall stand in thy way: but all that thou desirest shall be there together present, and shall replenish thy whole affection, and shall satiate it to the full.

There I will give thee glory for the affronts which thou hast suffered; a garment of praise for thy sorrow; and for thy having been seated here in the lowest place, a royal throne for all eternity.

There will the fruit of obedience appear, there will the labour of penance rejoice, and humble subjection shall be gloriously crowned.

7. Bow down thyself then humbly at present under the hands of all; and heed not who it was that has said or commanded this;

But let it be thy great care, that whether thy superior or inferior, or equal, desire any thing of thee, or hint at any thing, thou take all in good part, and labour with a sincere will to perform it.

Let one man seek this, another that; let this man glory in this thing, another in that, and be praised a thousand thousand times: but thou, for thy part, rejoice neither in this nor in that, but in the contempt of thyself, and in my good pleasure and honour alone.

This is what thou oughtest to wish, that whether in life, or in death, God may be always glorified in thee.

CHAPTER L.
HOW A DESOLATE PERSON OUGHT TO OFFER HIMSELF INTO THE HANDS OF GOD.

1. O Lord God, O Holy Father, be thou now and for ever blessed, for as thou wilt, so it has happened; and what thou dost is always good.

Let thy servant rejoice in thee, not in himself, nor in any other; for thou alone art true joy, thou my hope, and my crown; thou my gladness, and my honour, O Lord.

What hath thy servant but what he hath received from thee, and this without any merit on his side? All things are thine which thou hast given, and which thou hast made.

I am poor, and in my labours from my youth; and my soul is grieved even unto tears sometimes; and sometimes is disturbed within herself by reason of the passions which encompass her.

2. I long for the joy of peace, I beg for the peace of thy children, who are fed by thee in the light of thy consolation.

If thou givest peace, if thou infusest holy joy, the soul of thy servant shall be full of melody, and devout in thy praise.

But if thou withdraw thyself, as thou art very often accustomed to do, he will not be able to run in the way of thy commandments; but rather must bow down his knees, and knock his breast, because it is not with him, as it was yesterday and the day before, when thy lamp shined over his head, and he was covered under the shadow of thy wings from temptation rushing in upon him.

3. O just Father, holy, and always to be praised, the hour is come for thy servant to be tried.

O Father, worthy of all love, it is fitting that thy servant should at this hour suffer something for thee.

O Father, always to be honoured, the hour is come, when thou didst foresee from all eternity, that thy servant for the short time should be oppressed *without*, but always live *within* to thee; that he should be a little slighted, and humbled, and should fall in the sight of men; that he should be severely afflicted with sufferings and diseases; that so he may rise again with thee in the dawning of a new light, and be glorified in heaven.

O holy Father, thou hast so appointed, and such is thy will; and that has come to pass which thou hast ordered.

4. For this is a favour to thy friend, that he should suffer and be afflicted in this world for the love of thee; how often soever, and by whomsoever thou permittest it to fall upon him.

Without thy counsel and providence, and without cause nothing is done upon earth.

It is good for me, O Lord, that thou hast humbled me, that I may learn thy justifications, (Psalms cxviii.) and cast away from me all pride of heart and presumption.

[USCCB: Psalms cxix. 71. "It was good for me to be afflicted, in order to learn your laws."]

It is advantageous for me that shame has covered my face, that I may rather seek my comfort from thee, than from men.

I have also learned hereby to fear thy impenetrable judgment, who afflicting the just together with the wicked, but not without equity and justice.

5. Thanks be to thee, that thou hast not spared me in my evils, but hast bruised me with bitter stripes, inflicting pains, and sending distress both within and without.

And of all things under heaven, there is none can comfort me but thou, O Lord my God, the heavenly physician of souls, *who woundest and healest, bringest down to hell, and leadest back again.*

Thy discipline is on me, and thy rod shall instruct me.

6. Behold, dear Father, I am in thy hands, I bow myself down under the rod of thy correction.

Strike thou my back and my neck, that I may bend my crookedness to thy will:

Make me a pious and humble disciple of thine, as thou art wont well to do, that I may walk at thy beck at all times.

To thee I commit myself and all that is mine, to be corrected by thee: it is better to be chastised here than hereafter.

Thou knowest all and every thing, and there is nothing in man's conscience hidden from thee.

Thou knowest things to come, before they are done; and thou hast no need to be taught or admonished by any one of these things that pass upon earth.

Thou knowest what is expedient for my progress, and how serviceable tribulation is to rub away the rust of sin.

Do with me according to thy good pleasure, it is what I desire, and despise not my sinful life, to no one better or more clearly known than to thyself alone.

7. Grant, O Lord, that I may know what I ought to know; that I may love what I ought to love; that I may praise that which is most pleasing to thee; that I may esteem that which is valuable in thy sight; that I may despise that which is despicable in thy eyes.

Suffer me not to judge according to the sight of the outward eye, nor to give sentence according to the hearing of the ears of men that know not what they are about: but to determine both of visible and spiritual matters with *true* judgment, and above all things ever to seek thy good-will and pleasure.

8. The sentiments of men are often wrong in their judgments; and the lovers of this world are deceived in loving visible things alone;

What is a man the better for being reputed greater by man?

One deceitful man deceives another; the vain deceives the vain, the blind deceives the blind, the weak the weak, whilst he extols him;

And in truth doth rather confound him whilst he vainly praiseth him: for how much each one is in thy eyes, so much is he, and no more, saith the humble St. Francis.

CHAPTER LI.
THAT WE MUST PRACTISE OURSELVES IN HUMBLE WORKS, WHEN WE CANNOT ATTAIN TO HIGH THINGS.

1. Son, thou must not always continue in the most fervent desire of virtues, nor stand in the highest degree of contemplation; but it must needs be that thou sometimes descend to lower things, by reason of original corruption; and that thou bear the burden of this corruptible life, even against thy will, and with irksomeness.

As long as thou carriest about with thee thy mortal body, thou shalt feel trouble and heaviness of heart.

Thou oughtest therefore, as long as thou art in the flesh, oftentimes to bewail the burden of the flesh; for that thou canst not without intermission be employed in spiritual exercises and divine contemplation.

2. At these times it is expedient for thee to fly to humble and exterior works, and to recreate thyself in good actions; to look for my coming and heavenly visitation with an assured hope; to bear with patience thy banishment, and the aridity of thy mind, till thou be visited again by me, and delivered from all anguish.

For I will make thee forget thy pains, and enjoy eternal rest.

I will lay open before thee the pleasant fields of the scriptures, that thy heart being dilated, thou mayest begin to run the way of my commandments.

And that thou shalt say, the sufferings of this time have no proportion with the future glory, which shall be revealed in us. Romans viii.

CHAPTER LII.
THAT A MAN OUGHT NOT TO ESTEEM HIMSELF WORTHY OF CONSOLATION; BUT RATHER GUILTY OF STRIPES.

1. Lord, I am not worthy of thy consolation, or any spiritual visitation; and therefore thou dealest justly with me, when thou leavest me poor and desolate.

For if I could shed tears like a sea, yet should I not be worthy of thy comfort;

Since I have deserved nothing but stripes and punishments, because I have grievously and often offended thee, and in very many things sinned against thee.

Therefore according to all just reason I have not deserved the least of thy comforts.

But thou, who art a good and merciful God, who wilt not have thy works perish, to shew the riches of thy goodness towards the vessels of mercy, vouchsafest beyond all his deserts to comfort thy servant above human measure; for thy consolations are not like the consolations of men.

2. What have I done, O Lord, that thou shouldst impart any heavenly comfort to me?

I can remember nothing of good that ever I have done; but that I was always prone to vice, and sluggish to amendment.

It is the truth, and I cannot deny it. If I should say otherwise, thou wouldst stand against me, and there would be none to defend me.

What have I deserved for my sins but hell and everlasting fire?

In truth, I confess I am worthy of all scorn and contempt; neither is it fitting that I should be named among thy devout servants. And though it goes against me to hear this, yet for truth's sake I will condemn my sins against myself, that so I may the easier obtain thy mercy.

3. What shall I say, who am guilty, and full of all confusion?

I have not the face to say any thing but this one word, I have sinned, O Lord, I have sinned; have mercy on me, and pardon me.

Suffer me a little, that I may mourn out my grief, before I go to the darksome land that is covered with the dismal shade of death. Job x.

What dost thou chiefly require of a guilty and wretched sinner, but that he should heartily repent, and humble himself for his sins.

In true contrition and humility of heart is brought forth hope of forgiveness; a troubled conscience is reconciled; grace that was lost is recovered; a man is secured from the wrath to come, and God meets the penitent soul in the holy kiss of peace.

4. Humble contrition for sins is an acceptable sacrifice to thee, O Lord; of far sweeter odour in thy sight than the burning of frankincense.

This is also that pleasing ointment which thou wouldst have to be poured upon thy sacred feet: *for thou never yet hast despised a contrite and humble heart*. Psalms l.

> [USCCB: Psalms li. 19. "...God, do not spurn
> a broken, humbled heart."]

Here is a sure place of refuge from the face of the wrath of the enemy: here whatever has been elsewhere contracted of uncleanness is amended and washed away.

CHAPTER LIII.
THAT THE GRACE OF GOD IS NOT COMMUNICATED TO THE EARTHLY MINDED.

1. Son, my grace is precious; it suffers not itself to be mingled with external things, or earthly consolations.

Thou must therefore cast away all impediments of grace, if thou desire to have it infused into thee.

Choose a secret place to thyself; love to dwell with thyself alone; seek not to be talking with any one; but rather pour forth devout prayers to God, that thou mayest keep thy mind in compunction, and thy conscience clean.

Esteem the whole world as nothing: prefer the attendance on God before all external things:

For thou canst not both attend to me, and at the same time delight thyself in transitory things.

Thou must be sequestered from thy acquaintance, and from those that are dear to thee, and keep thy mind disengaged from all temporal comfort.

So the blessed apostle Peter beseeches the faithful of Christ to keep themselves *as strangers and pilgrims in this world*. 1 Peter ii.

2. Oh! how great confidence shall he have at the hour of his death, who is not detained by an affection to any thing in the world?

But an infirm soul is not yet capable of having a heart thus perfectly disengaged from all things; neither doth the sensual man understand the liberty of an internal man.

But if he will be *spiritual* indeed, he must renounce as well those that are near him, as those that are afar off; and beware of none more than of himself.

If thou perfectly overcome thyself, thou shalt with more ease subdue all things else.

The perfect victory is to triumph over one's self.

For he that keeps himself in subjection, so that his sensuality is ever subject to reason, and reason in all things obedient to me, he is indeed a conqueror of himself, and Lord of all the world.

3. If thou desire to mount thus high, thou must begin manfully, and set the axe to the root, that thou mayest root out and destroy thy secret inordinate inclination to thyself, and to all selfish and earthly goods.

This vice, by which a man inordinately loves himself, is at the bottom of all that which is to be rooted out and overcome in us; which evil being once conquered and brought under, a great peace and tranquillity will presently ensue.

But because there are few that labour to die perfectly to themselves, and that fully tend beyond themselves; therefore do they remain entangled in themselves, nor can they be elevated in spirit above themselves.

But he that desires to walk freely with me, must mortify all his wicked and irregular affections, and must not cleave to any thing created with any concupiscence or private love.

CHAPTER LIV.
OF THE DIFFERENT MOTIONS OF NATURE AND GRACE.

1. Son, observe diligently the motions of **nature** and **grace**; for they move very opposite ways, and very subtilly; and can hardly be distinguished but by a spiritual man, and one that is internally illuminated.

All men indeed aim at **good**, and pretend to something of good in what they do and say; therefore, under the appearance of good many are deceived.

2. **Nature** is crafty, and draws away many, ensnares them and deceives them, and always intends herself for her end:

But **grace** walks with simplicity, declines from all shew of evil, offers no deceits, and does all things purely for God, in whom also she rests, as in her last end.

3. **Nature** is not willing to be mortified, or to be restrained, or to be overcome, or to be subject; neither will she of her own accord be brought under:

But **grace** studies the mortification of her own self, resists sensuality, seeks to be subject, covets to be overcome, aims not at following her own liberty, loves to be kept under discipline, and desires not to have the command over any one; but under God ever to live, stand, and be; and for God's sake is ever ready humbly to bow down herself under all human creatures.

4. **Nature** labours for her own interest, and considers what gain she may reap from another:

But **grace** considers not what may be advantageous and profitable to herself; but rather what may be profitable to many.

5. **Nature** willingly receives honour and respect:

But **grace** faithfully attributes all honour and glory to God.

6. **Nature** is afraid of being put to shame and despised:

But **grace** is glad to suffer reproach for the name of Jesus.

7. **Nature** loves idleness and bodily rest:

But **grace** cannot be idle, and willingly embraces labour.

8. **Nature** seeks to have things that are curious and fine, and does not care for things that are cheap and coarse:

But **grace** is pleased with that which is plain and humble, rejects not coarse things, nor refuses to be clad in old clothes.

9. **Nature** has regard to temporal things, rejoices at earthly gain, is troubled at losses, and is provoked at every slight injurious word:

But **grace** attends to things eternal, and cleaves not to those which pass with time; neither is she disturbed at the loss of things, nor exasperated with hard words; for she places her treasure and her joy in heaven, where nothing is lost.

10. **Nature** is covetous, and is more willing to take than to give; and loves to have things to herself:

But **grace** is bountiful and open-hearted, avoids selfishness, is contented with little, and judges it *more happy to give than to receive*. Acts xx.

11. **Nature** inclines to creatures, to her own flesh, to vanities, and to gadding abroad:

But **grace** draws to God, and virtues; renounces creatures, flies the world, hates the desires of the flesh, restrains wandering about, and is ashamed to appear in public.

12. *Nature* willingly receives exterior comfort: in which she may be sensibly delighted:

But *grace* seeks to be comforted in God alone, and beyond all things visible to be delighted in the Sovereign Good.

13. *Nature* doth all for her own lucre and interest; she can do nothing *gratis*, but hopes to gain sometime equal, or better, or praise or favour for her good deeds; and covets to have her actions and gifts much valued:

But *grace* seeks nothing temporal; nor requires any other recompence but God alone for her reward; nor desires any more of the necessaries of this life than may be serviceable for the obtaining of a happy eternity.

14. *Nature* rejoices in a multitude of friends and kindred; she glories in the nobility of her stock and descent; she fawns on them that are in power, flatters the rich, and applauds such as are like herself:

But *grace* loves even her enemies, and is not puffed up with having a great many friends, nor has any value for family or birth, unless when joined with greater virtue; she rather favours the poor than the rich; she has more compassion for the innocent than the powerful; she rejoices with him that loves the truth, and not with the deceitful; she ever exhorts the good to be zealous for better gifts, and to become like to the Son of God by the exercise of virtues.

15. *Nature* easily complains of want, and of trouble:

But *grace* bears poverty with constancy.

16. *Nature* turns all things to herself, and for herself she labours and disputes:

But *grace* refers all things to God, from whom all originally proceed; she attributes no good to herself, nor does she arrogantly presume of herself; she does not contend, nor prefer her own opinion to others; but in every sense and understanding she submits herself to the Eternal Wisdom, and to the divine examination.

17. *Nature* covets to know secrets, and to hear news; is willing to appear abroad, and to have the experience of many things by the senses; desires to be taken notice of, and to do such things as may procure praise and admiration:

But *grace* cares not for the hearing of news or curious things, because all this springs from the old corruption, since nothing is new or lasting upon earth:

She teaches therefore to restrain the senses, to avoid vain complacence and ostentation, humbly to hide those things which are worthy of praise and admiration; and from every thing, and in every knowledge, to seek the fruit of spiritual profit, and the praise and honour of God:

She desires not to have herself, or what belongs to her, extolled; but wishes that God may be blessed in his gifts, who bestows all out of mere love.

18. This *grace* is a supernatural light, and a certain special gift of God, and the proper mark of the elect, and pledge of eternal salvation, which elevates a man from the things of the earth to the love of heavenly things, and of carnal makes him spiritual:

By how much therefore the more *nature* is kept down and subdued, with so much the greater abundance *grace* is infused; and the inward man, by new visitations, is daily more reformed according to the image of God.

CHAPTER LV.
OF THE CORRUPTION OF NATURE, AND OF THE EFFICACY OF DIVINE GRACE.

1. O Lord, my God, who hast created me to thy own image and likeness, grant me this **grace**, which thou hast declared to be so great, and so necessary to salvation; that I may overcome my wicked **nature**, which draws to sin and perdition:

For I perceive in my flesh the law of sin contradicting the law of my mind, and leading me captive to obey sensuality in many things; neither can I resist the passions thereof, unless thy most holy **grace** assist me, infused ardently into my heart.

2. I stand in need of thy **grace**, and of a great **grace** to overcome **nature**, which is always prone to evil from her youth;

For she having fallen in Adam, the first man, and having been corrupted by sin, the penalty of this stain has descended upon all mankind: so that **nature** itself, which by thee was created good and right, is now put for the vice and infirmity of corrupt nature; because the motion thereof, left to itself, draws to evil, and to things below;

For the little strength which remains, is but like a spark hidden in the ashes.

This is our **natural reason**, which is surrounded with a great mist, having yet the judgment of good and evil, and of the distance of truth and falsehood; though it be unable to fulfil all that it approves; neither does it now enjoy the full light of truth, nor the former integrity of its affections.

3. Hence it is, O my God, that according to the inward man I am delighted with thy law, knowing thy command to be good, just, and holy, and reproving all evil and sin, as what ought to be shunned:

And yet in the flesh I serve the law of sin, whilst I rather obey sensuality than reason.

Hence it is, that to will good is present with me, but how to accomplish it I do not find. Romans vii.

Hence I often make many good purposes; but because I want grace to help my weakness, through a slight resistance, I recoil and fall off.

Hence it comes to pass, that I know the way to perfection, and see clearly enough what it is I ought to do;

But being pressed down with the weight of my own corruption, I rise not to those things which are more perfect.

4. O how exceedingly necessary is thy **grace** for me, O Lord, to begin that which is good, to go forward with it, and to accomplish it? For without it I can do nothing: but I can do all things in thee, when thy grace strengthens me.

O truly heavenly grace, without which we have no merits of our own, neither are any of the gifts of nature to be valued!

No arts, no riches, no beauty or strength, no wit or eloquence, are of any worth with thee, O Lord, without grace;

For the gifts of nature are common to the good and bad: but grace or divine love is the proper gift of the elect, which they that are adorned with are esteemed worthy of eternal life.

This grace is so excellent, that neither the gift of prophecy, nor the working of miracles, nor any speculation, how sublime soever, is of any value without it.

Nor even faith, nor hope, nor any other virtues, are acceptable to thee, without charity and grace.

5. O most blessed grace, which makest the poor in spirit rich in virtues, and renderest him that is rich in many good things humble of heart;

Come, descend upon me, replenish me betimes with consolation, lest my soul faint through weariness and dryness of mind.

I beg of thee, O Lord, that I may find *grace* in thy sight; for thy *grace* is enough for me, though I obtain none of those things which nature desires.

If I be tempted and afflicted with many tribulations, I will fear no evil, whilst thy *grace* is with me;

She is my strength; she gives counsel and help;

She is more mighty than all my enemies, and wiser than all the wise.

6. She is the mistress of truth, the teacher of discipline, the light of the heart, the comfort in affliction, the banisher of sorrow, the expeller of fear, the nurse of devotion, the producer of tears.

What am I without her but a piece of dry wood, and an unprofitable stock, fit for nothing but to be cast away!

Let thy grace therefore, O Lord, always both go before me and follow me, and make me ever intent upon good works, through Jesus Christ, thy Son. **Amen**.

CHAPTER LVI.
THAT WE OUGHT TO DENY OURSELVES, AND TO IMITATE CHRIST BY THE CROSS.

1. Son, as much as thou canst go out of thyself, so much wilt thou be able to enter into me.

As the desiring of nothing abroad brings peace at home, so the relinquishing ourselves interiorly joins us to God.

I will have thee learn the perfect renouncing of thyself in my will, without contradiction or complaint.

Follow me, *I am the way, the truth and the life*. John xiv. Without the *way* there is no going; without the *truth* there is no knowing; without the *life* there is no living.

I am *the way* which thou must follow; *the truth*, which thou must believe; *the life*, which thou must hope for.

I am *the way* inviolable, *the truth* infallible, and *the life* that has no end.

I am the straitest *way*, the sovereign *truth*, the true *life*, a blessed *life*, an uncreated *life*.

If thou abide in my *way*, thou shalt know the *truth*, and the *truth* shall deliver thee, and thou shalt attain to *life* everlasting.

2. If thou wilt enter into life, keep the commandments. Luke ix.

> [USCCB: Matthew xix. 17. "If you wish to
> enter into life, keep the commandments."]

If thou wilt know the truth, believe me: If thou wilt be perfect, sell all:

It thou wilt be my disciple, deny thyself:

If thou wilt possess a blessed life, despise this present life:

If thou wilt be exalted in heaven, humble thyself in this world:

If thou wilt reign with me, bear the cross with me:

For none but the servants of the cross find the way of bliss and of true light.

3. Lord Jesus, forasmuch as thy way is narrow, and despised by the world; grant that I may follow thee, and be despised by the world:

For the servant is not greater than his Lord, neither is the disciple above his master. *Matthew* vi.

> [USCCB: Matthew x. 24. "No disciple is above
> his teacher, no slave above his master."]

Let thy servant meditate on thy life, for there is my salvation and true holiness:

Whatever I read, or hear besides, does not recreate nor fully delight me.

4. Son, thou knowest these things, and hast read them all, happy shalt thou be if thou fulfil them.

He that hath my commandments and keepeth them, he it is that loveth me; and I will love him, and I will manifest myself unto him, (John xiv.); and I will make him to sit with me in the kingdom of my Father. Apoc. iii.

5. Lord Jesus, as thou hast said and hast promised, so may it be indeed; and may it be my lot to merit it:

I have received the cross, I have received it from thy hand; and I will bear it, and bear it till death, as thou hast laid it upon me. Indeed the life of a good religious man is a cross, but it is a cross that conducts him to Paradise:

We have now begun, it is not lawful to go back, nor may we leave off.

6. Take courage, my brethren, let us go forward together, Jesus will be with us:

For Jesus's sake we took up this cross; for Jesus's sake let us persevere in it.

He will be our helper, who is our captain and our leader.

Behold our king marches before us, who will fight for us.

Let us follow him like men of courage; let no one shrink through fear; let us be ready valiantly to die in battle, and not to suffer our glory to be blemished by flying from the standard of the cross.

CHAPTER LVII.
THAT A MAN SHOULD NOT BE TOO MUCH DEJECTED WHEN HE FALLS INTO SOME DEFECTS.

1. Son, patience and humility in adversity are more pleasing to me, than much consolation and devotion in prosperity.

Why art thou disturbed at a little thing said against thee?

If it had been more, thou oughtest not to be moved.

But now let it pass, it is not the first, or any thing new, nor will it be the last, if thou live long.

Thou art valiant enough, as long as no adversary or opposition comes in thy way:

Thou canst also give good advice, and encourage others with thy words: but when any unexpected trouble comes to knock at thy door, then thy counsel and thy courage fails thee.

Consider thy great frailty, which thou often experiencest in small difficulties. Yet it is done for thy good, as often as these or such like things befal thee.

2. Put it out of thy heart the best thou canst; and if it had touched thee, yet let it not cast thee down, nor keep thee a long time entangled.

At least bear it patiently, if thou canst not receive it with joy.

And though thou be not willing to hear it, and perceivest an indignation arising within thyself, yet repress thyself, and suffer no inordinate word to come out of thy mouth which may scandalize the weak.

The commotion which is stirred up in thee will quickly be allayed, and thy inward pain will be sweetened by the return of grace.

I am still living, saith the Lord, ready to help thee, and comfort thee more than before, if thou put thy trust in me, and devoutly call upon me.

3. Keep thy mind calm and even, and prepare thyself for bearing still more.

All is not lost, if thou feel thyself often afflicted or grievously tempted:

Thou art man and not God, thou art flesh and not an angel.

How canst thou look to continue ever in the same state of virtue, when this was not found in the angels in heaven, nor in the first man in Paradise?

I am he that raises up, and saves them that mourn; and them that know their own infirmity I advance to my divinity.

4. O Lord, blessed be this thy word, it is more sweet to my mouth than honey, and the honey-comb.

What shall I do in my so great tribulations and anguishes, didst thou not encourage me with thy holy words?

What matter is it how much or what I suffer, so I come but at length to the haven of salvation.

Grant me a good end, grant me a happy passage out of this world:

Be ever mindful of me, O my God, and direct me by this strait road to thy kingdom. **Amen**.

CHAPTER LVIII.
OF NOT SEARCHING INTO HIGH MATTERS, NOR INTO THE SECRET JUDGMENTS OF GOD.

1. Son, see thou dispute not of high matters, nor of the hidden judgments of God; why this man is left thus, and this other is raised to so great grace; or why this person is so much afflicted, and that other so highly exalted.

These things are above the reach of man, neither can any reason or discourse be able to penetrate into the judgments of God.

When therefore the enemy suggests to thee such things as these, or thou hearest curious men inquiring into them, answer that of the prophet, *Thou art just, O Lord, and thy judgment is right.* Psalms cxviii.

[USCCB: Psalms cxix. 137. "You are righteous, LORD, and just are your edicts."]

And again: The judgments of the Lord are true, justified in themselves. Psalms xviii.

[USCCB: Psalms xix. 8, 9. "The law of the LORD is perfect, refreshing the soul. The decree of the LORD is trustworthy, giving wisdom to the simple. The precepts of the LORD are right, rejoicing the heart. The command of the LORD is clear, enlightening the eye."]

My judgments are to be feared, not to be searched into, for they are incomprehensible to human understanding.

2. In like manner do not inquire nor dispute of the merits of the saints, which of them is more holy than the other, or which greater in the kingdom of heaven.

These things oftentimes breed strife and unprofitable contentions, and nourish pride and vain-glory; from whence arise envy and dissensions, whilst this man proudly seeks to prefer this saint, and another man is for preferring another.

Now to desire to know and to search into such things as these, is of no profit, but rather displeaseth the saints; for *I am not the God of dissensions, but of peace* (1 Corinthians xiv.), which peace consists more in true humility than in exalting one's self.

3. Some are carried by a zeal of love towards these, or those, with greater affection; but this affection is rather human than divine.

I am he who made all the saints; I gave them grace, I have brought them to glory.

I know the merits of every one of them, I prevented them by the blessings of my sweetness.

I foreknew my beloved ones before the creation: I chose them out of the world, they were not before-hand with me to chuse me;

I called them by my grace, and drew them to me by my mercy. I led them safe through many temptations, I imparted to them extraordinary comforts, I gave them perseverance, I have crowned their patience.

4. I know the first and the last, I embrace them all with an inestimable love.

I am to be praised in all my saints, I am to be blessed above all things, and to be honoured in every one of them whom I have thus gloriously magnified, and eternally chosen without any foregoing merits of their own.

He therefore that despises one of the least of my saints, honours not the greatest, for both little and great I have made:

And he that derogates from any one of the saints, derogates also from me, and from all the rest of them in the kingdom of heaven.

They are all one through the band of love; they have the same sentiment, the same will, and all mutually love one another.

5. And yet (which is much higher) they all love me more than themselves and their own merit.

For being elevated above themselves, and drawn out of the love of themselves, they are wholly absorpt in the love of me, in whom also they rest by an eternal enjoyment.

Nor is there any thing which can divert them from me, or depress them; for being full of the eternal truth, they burn with the fire of a charity that cannot be extinguished.

Therefore let carnal and sensual men (who know not how to affect any thing but their private satisfactions) forbear to dispute of the state of the saints: they add and take away according to their own inclination, and not according to what is pleasing to the everlasting truth.

6. In many there is ignorance, especially in such as being but little enlightened seldom know how to love any one with a perfect spiritual love.

They are as yet much inclined to such or such by a natural affection and human friendship; and as they are affected with regard to things below, they conceive the like imaginations of the things of heaven.

But there is an incomparable distance between what the imperfect imagine, and what enlightened men contemplate by revelation from above.

7. Take heed, therefore, my Son, that thou treat not curiously of those things which exceed thy knowledge, but rather make it thy business and thy aim, that thou mayest be found, though it were the least, in the kingdom of God.

And if any one should know who were more holy or greater in the kingdom of heaven, what would the knowledge profit him, unless he would take occasion from knowing this to humble himself in my sight, and to praise my name with greater fervour?

It is much more acceptable to God for a man to think of the greatness of his own sins, and how little he is in virtues, and at how great a distance he is from the perfection of the saints, than to dispute which of them is greater or less.

It is better to invoke the saints with devout prayers and tears, and to implore their glorious suffrages with an humble mind, than by a vain inquiry to search into their secrets.

8. They are well and perfectly contented, if men would be but contented, and refrain from their vain discourses.

They glory not of their own merits, for they ascribe nothing of goodness to themselves, but all to me; because I bestowed all upon them out of my infinite charity.

They are filled with so great a love of the Deity, and such overflowing joy, that there is nothing wanting to their glory, nor can any happiness be wanting to them.

All the saints by how much they are the higher in glory, by so much are they the more humble in themselves, and nearer to me, and better beloved by me.

And therefore thou hast it written, that they cast down their crowns before God, and fell upon their faces before the lamb, and adored him that lives for ever and ever. Apoc. iv.

9. Many examine who is greatest in the kingdom of God, who know not whether they shall be worthy to be numbered amongst the least.

It is a great matter to be even the least in heaven, where all are great; because all shall be called the children of God:

The least shall be as a thousand, and a sinner of an hundred years shall die.

For when the disciples asked, **Who was the greatest in the kingdom of heaven?** (Matthew xviii.) they received this answer:

Unless you be converted and become as little children, you shall not enter into the kingdom of heaven. Whosoever therefore shall humble himself as this little one, he is the greatest in the kingdom of heaven.

10. Woe to them who disdain to humble themselves willingly with little children; for the low gate of the heavenly kingdom will not suffer them to enter thither.

Woe also to the rich who have their comforts here, for when the poor shall go into the kingdom of God, they stand lamenting without.

Rejoice you humble, and be glad you that are poor, for yours is the kingdom of God; yet so, if you walk in the truth.

CHAPTER LIX.
THAT ALL HOPE AND CONFIDENCE IS TO BE FIXED IN GOD ALONE.

1. Lord, what is my confidence which I have in this life? or what is my greatest comfort amongst all things that appear under heaven?

Is it not thou, my Lord God, whose mercies are without number?

Where was it ever well with me without thee? or when could it be ill with me when thou wast present?

I had rather be poor for thee, than rich without thee.

I chuse rather to sojourn on earth with thee, than to possess heaven without thee. Where thou art, there is heaven: and there is death and hell, where thou art not.

After thee I have a longing desire, and therefore I must needs sigh after thee, and cry and pray.

In fine, I cannot fully trust in any one to bring me seasonable help in my necessities, save only in thee, my God.

Thou art my hope, thou art my confidence, thou art my comforter, and most faithful above all.

2. All seek their own interest; thou aimest only at my salvation and profit, and turnest all things to my good.

And although thou expose me to various temptations and adversities, yet all this thou ordainest for my good, who art wont to prove thy beloved servants a thousand ways:

Under which proofs, thou oughtest no less to be loved and praised, than if thou wert to fill me with heavenly comforts.

3. In thee, therefore, O Lord God, I put all my hope and refuge; in thee I place all my tribulation and anguish; for I find all to be infirm and unstable whatever I behold out of thee.

For neither will a multitude of friends be of any service to me, nor can strong auxiliaries bring me any succours, nor wise counsellors give me a profitable answer, nor the books of the learned comfort me, nor any wealth deliver me, nor any secret and pleasant place secure me, if thou thyself do not assist; help, strengthen, comfort, instruct and defend me.

4. For all things which seem to be for our peace and for our happiness, when thou art absent, are nothing, and in truth contribute nothing to our felicity.

Thou therefore art the fountain of all good, and the height of life, and the depth of wisdom; and to trust in thee above all things is the strongest comfort of thy servants.

To thee I lift up mine eyes; in thee, O my God; the Father of mercies, I put my trust:

Bless and sanctify my soul with thy heavenly blessing, that it may be made thy holy habitation, and the seat of thy eternal glory; and let nothing be found in the temple of thy dignity that may offend the eyes of thy Majesty.

According to the greatness of thy goodness, and the multitude of thy tender mercies, look down upon me, and give ear to the prayer of thy poor servant, who is in banishment afar off from thee in the region of the shade of death.

Protect and defend the soul of thy servant amidst so many of this corruptible life; and direct him in the company of thy grace, through the way of peace to the country of everlasting light. **Amen.**

End Of Book III.

THE IMITATION OF CHRIST.

BOOK IV.

The Voice Of Christ.

Come to me all you that labour, and are heavy burthened, and I will refresh you, saith the Lord. Matthew xi.

The bread which I will give, is my flesh, for the life of the world. John vi.

Take and eat, This is my body, which shall be delivered for you: do this in remembrance of me. 1 Corinthians xi.

He that eateth my flesh, and drinketh my blood, abideth in me, and I in him. John vi.

The words which I have spoken to you are spirit and life. John vi.

CHAPTER I.
WITH HOW GREAT REVERENCE CHRIST IS TO BE RECEIVED.

The Voice of the Disciple.

1. These are thy words, O Christ, the Eternal Truth, though not all delivered at one time, nor written in one place.

Since therefore they are thy words, and they are true, they are all to be received by me with thanks, and with faith.

They are thine, and thou hast spoken them; and they are also mine, because thou hast delivered them for my salvation.

I willingly receive them from thy mouth, that they may be more inseparably ingrafted in my heart.

These words of so great tenderness, full of sweetness and love, encourage me; but my own sins terrify me, and my unclean conscience keeps me back from approaching to so great mysteries.

The sweetness of thy words invites me, but the multitude of my offence weighs me down.

2. Thou commandest me to approach to thee with confidence, if I would have part with thee, and to receive the food of immortality, if I desire to obtain life, and glory everlasting.

Come, sayest thou, to me all you that labour, and are heavy burthened, and I will refresh you. Matthew xi.

O sweet and amiable word in the ear of a sinner, that thou, O Lord my God, shouldst invite the poor and needy to the communion of thy most sacred body!

But who am I, O Lord, that I should presume to come to thee?

Behold, the heavens of heavens cannot contain thee; and thou sayest, *Come you all unto me*.

3. What means this most loving condescension, and so friendly an invitation?

How shall I dare to approach, who am conscious to myself of no good, on which I can presume?

How shall I introduce thee into my house, who have oftentimes offended thy most gracious countenance?

The angels and archangels stand with a reverential awe, the saints and the just are afraid; and thou sayest, *Come you all unto me*.

Unless thou, O Lord, didst say it, who could believe it to be true?

And unless thou didst command it, who would dare attempt to approach?

4. Behold Noah, a just man, laboured a hundred years in building of the ark, that he with a few might be preserved; and how shall I be able in the space of one hour to prepare myself to receive with reverence the Maker of the world?

Moses, thy servant, thy great and special friend, made an ark of incorruptible wood, which he also covered with most pure gold, that he might reposite therein the tables of the law; and shall I, a rotten creature, presume so easily to receive thee the Maker of the law, and Giver of life?

Solomon, the wisest of the kings of Israel, employed seven years in building a magnificent temple for the praise of thy name;

And for eight days together he celebrated the feast of the dedication thereof: he offered a thousand pacific victims, and brought in the ark of the covenant in a solemn manner, into the place prepared for it, with the sound of trumpet and jubilee:

And I, a wretch, and the vilest of men, how shall I bring thee into my house, who can hardly spend one half hour devoutly? and would to God I had ever once spent one half hour as I ought!

5. O, my God, how much did they endeavour to do to please thee?

Alas! how little it is that I do! How short a time do I spend when I prepare myself to communicate? Seldom am I wholly recollected, very seldom free from all distraction;

And yet surely, in the life-giving presence of thy Deity, no unbecoming thought should occur, nor any thing created take up my mind; for it is not an angel, but the Lord of angels, that I am to entertain.

6. And yet there is a very great difference between the ark of the covenant with its relics, and thy most pure body with its unspeakable virtues; between those sacrifices of the law, which were figures of things to come, and the true sacrifice of thy body, which is the accomplishing of all those ancient sacrifices.

7. Why then am I not more inflamed, considering thy venerable presence?

Why do I not prepare myself with greater care to receive thy sacred gifts, seeing that these ancient holy patriarchs and prophets, yea kings also and princes, with the whole people, have shewn so great affection of devotion towards the divine worship?

8. The most devout King David danced before the ark of God with all his force, commemorating the benefits bestowed in times past on the Fathers. He made musical instruments of sundry kinds; he published psalms, and appointed them to be sung with joy; he himself likewise often sung them playing upon his harp, inspired with the grace of the Holy Ghost: he taught the people of Israel to praise God with their whole heart, and to join their voices in blessing and magnifying him every day.

If so great devotion was then used, and such remembrance of the praise of God before the ark of the covenant; how great ought to be the reverence and devotion which I, and all Christian people, should have in the presence of this sacrament, in the receiving the most excellent body of Christ?

9. Many run to sundry places to visit the relics of the saints, and are astonished to hear their wonderful works; they behold the noble buildings of their churches, and kiss their sacred bones wrapt up in silk and gold;

And, behold, I have thee here present on the altar, my God, the Saint of saints, the Creator of men, and the Lord of angels.

Oftentimes in seeing those things men are moved with curiosity, and the novelty of the sight, and but little fruit of amendment is reaped thereby; especially when persons lightly run hither and thither, without true contrition for their sins:

But here, in the sacrament of the altar, thou art wholly present, my God and man, Christ Jesus; where also the fruit of eternal salvation is plentifully reaped, as often as thou art worthily and devoutly received.

And to this we are not drawn by any levity, curiosity, or sensuality; but by a firm faith, a devout hope, and sincere charity.

10. O God, the invisible Maker of the world, how wonderfully dost thou deal with us? How sweetly and graciously dost thou order all things in favour of thy elect, to whom thou offerest thyself to be received in the sacrament?

For this exceeds all understanding of man; this, in a particular manner, engages the hearts of the devout, and enkindles their love.

For thy true faithful, who dispose their whole life to amendment, by this most worthy sacrament, frequently receive a great grace of devotion and love of virtue.

11. Oh! the wonderful and hidden grace of this sacrament, which the faithful of Christ only know; but unbelievers, and such as are slaves to sin, cannot experience.

In this sacrament is conferred spiritual grace, and virtue lost is repaired in the soul; and beauty disfigured by sin returns again.

And so great sometimes is this grace, that from the abundance of the devotion that is bestowed, not only the mind but the frail body also feels a great increase of strength.

12. Yet it is much to be lamented and pitied, that we should be so lukewarm and negligent, as not to be drawn with greater affection to the receiving of Christ, in whom consists all the hope and merit of those that shall be saved:

For he is our sanctification, and our redemption; he is our comfort in our pilgrimage, and the saints' eternal enjoyment.

It is therefore much to be lamented that many take so little notice of this saving mystery, which rejoices heaven, and conserves the whole world.

Oh! the blindness and hardness of the heart of man, that doth not more consider so unspeakable a gift, and from the daily use of it falls into a disregard for it.

13. For if this most holy sacrament were only celebrated in one place, and consecrated by one only priest in the world, with how great desire dost thou think would men be affected to that place, and to such a priest of God, that they might see the divine mysteries celebrated?

But now there are made many priests, and Christ is offered up in many places, that the grace and love of God to man may appear by so much the greater, by how much this sacred communion is more spread throughout the world.

Thanks be to thee, O good Jesus, our eternal Shepherd, who hast vouchsafed to feed us poor exiles with thy precious body and blood, and to invite us to the receiving of these mysteries with the words of thy own mouth, saying; *Come to me all you that labour, and are burthened, and I will refresh you.* Matthew xi.

CHAPTER II.
THAT THE GREAT GOODNESS AND CHARITY OF GOD IS SHEWED TO MAN IN THIS SACRAMENT.

The Voice of the Disciple.

1. O Lord, trusting in thy goodness and in thy great mercy, I come sick to my Saviour, hungry and thirsty to the Fountain of Life, needy to the King of Heaven, a servant to his Lord, a creature to his Creator, and one in desolation to his loving Comforter.

But whence is this to me, that thou shouldst come to me? Who am I, that thou shouldst give me thyself?

How dare such a sinner appear before thee? and how dost thou vouchsafe to come to a sinner?

Thou knowest thy servant, and thou knowest that he has nothing of good in him which can entitle him to this favour.

I confess therefore my unworthiness, I acknowledge thy bounty, I praise thy goodness, and I give thee thanks for thy excessive charity:

For it is for thy own sake thou doest this, not for my merits, that thy goodness may be better known to me; that greater charity may be imparted, and humility more perfectly recommended.

Since therefore this is what pleaseth thee, and thou hast commanded it should be so, thy merciful condescension pleaseth me also; and I wish that my iniquity may be no obstacle.

2. Oh! most sweet and most bountiful Jesus, how great reverence and thanks, with perpetual praise, are due to thee for the receiving of thy sacred body, whose dignity no man can sufficiently express?

But what shall I think of in this communion, when I am approaching to my Lord, whom I can never reverence so much as I ought, and yet would gladly receive with devotion?

What can I think of better or more wholesome to my soul, than to humble myself entirely in thy presence, and extol thy infinite goodness above me?

I praise thee, O my God, and I extol thee for ever: I despise myself, and subject myself to thee, casting myself down to the depth of my unworthiness.

3. Behold, thou art the saint of saints, and I am the scum of sinners:

Behold, thou bowest thyself down to me, who am not worthy to look up to thee.

Behold, thou comest to me; thou art willing to be with me.

Thou invitest me to thy banquet, where thou wilt give me thy heavenly food, and the bread of angels to eat; no other, verily, than thyself, the living bread, who didst come down from heaven, and who givest life to the world.

4. Behold, whence love proceeds, what a bounty shines forth! how great thanks and praises are due to thee for these things!

Oh! how wholesome and profitable was thy device in this institution! how sweet and delightful this banquet in which thou givest thyself to be our food!

Oh! how admirable is thy work, O Lord! how powerful thy virtue! how infallible thy truth!

For thou hast spoken the word, and all things were made; and that has been done which thou hast commanded.

5. A wonderful thing it is, and worthy of faith, and exceeding all human understanding; that thou, O Lord, my God, true God, and true man, art contained whole and entire, under a small form of bread and wine, and without being consumed art eaten by the receiver.

Thou, the Lord of all things, who standest in need of no one, hast been pleased by this sacrament to dwell in us;

Preserve my heart and body without stain, that with a joyful and clean conscience I may be able often to celebrate thy sacred mysteries, and to receive for my eternal salvation what thou hast principally ordained and instituted for thy honour and perpetual remembrance.

6. Rejoice, O my soul, and give thanks to thy God for so noble a gift, and so singular a comfort, left to thee in this vale of tears.

For as often as thou repeatest this mystery, and receivest the body of Christ, so often dost thou celebrate the work of thy redemption, and art made partaker of all the merits of Christ;

For the charity of Christ is never diminished, and the greatness of his propitiation is never exhausted.

Therefore oughtest thou to dispose thyself for this, by perpetually renewing the vigour of thy mind, and to weigh with attentive consideration this great mystery of thy salvation.

And as often as thou sayest or hearest mass, it ought to seem to thee as great, new, and delightful, as if Christ that same day, first descending into the Virgin's womb, had been made man; or hanging on the cross was suffering and dying for the salvation of mankind.

CHAPTER III.
THAT IT IS PROFITABLE TO COMMUNICATE OFTEN.

The Voice of the Disciple.

1. Behold, I come to thee, O Lord, that it may be well with me by thy gift, and that I may be delighted in thy holy banquet, which thou, O God, in thy sweetness, hast prepared for the poor.

Behold, in thee is all whatsoever I can or ought to desire: thou art my salvation and redemption, my hope and my strength, my honour and my glory.

Make therefore the soul of thy servant joyful this day, because, O Lord Jesus, I have lifted up my soul to thee.

I desire at this time to receive thee devoutly and reverently; I would gladly bring thee into my house, that, like Zaccheus, I may receive thy blessing, and be numbered among the children of Abraham. *Luke* xix.

My soul longs after thy body; my heart aspires to be united with thee.

2. Give thyself to me, and it is enough; for besides thee no comfort is available.

Without thee I cannot subsist; and without thy visitation I cannot live;

And therefore I must come often to thee, and receive for the remedy of my soul's health; lest perhaps I faint in the way, if I be deprived of this heavenly food.

For so, O most merciful Jesus, thou wert pleased once to say, when thou hadst been preaching to the people, and curing sundry diseases, *I will not send them home fasting, lest they faint by the way*. Matthew xv.

Deal now in like manner with me, who hast left thyself in the sacrament for the comfort of thy faithful.

For thou art the most sweet refection of the soul, and he that shall eat thee worthily, shall be partaker and heir of everlasting glory.

It is indeed necessary for me (who am so often falling and committing sin, and so quickly grow slack and faint) by frequent prayers and confessions, and by the holy communion of thy body, to repair my strength, to cleanse and inflame myself, lest perhaps by abstaining for a longer time I fall away from my holy purpose.

3. For the senses of man are prone to evil from his youth; and unless thy divine medicine succour him, man quickly falls to worse.

The holy communion therefore withdraws him from evil, and strengthens him in good.

For if I am so often negligent and lukewarm now, when I communicate or celebrate, what would it be if I did not take this remedy, and should not seek so great a help?

And although I am not every day fit, nor well disposed to celebrate, yet I will endeavour at proper times to receive the divine mysteries, and to make myself partaker of so great a grace.

For this is the one principal comfort of a faithful soul, as long as she sojourns afar off from thee in this mortal body; being mindful often of her God, to receive her Beloved with a devout mind.

4. O wonderful condescension of thy tender love towards us, that thou, O Lord God, the Creator and Enlivener of all spirits, shouldst vouchsafe to come to a poor soul, and with thy whole divinity and humanity satisfy her hunger;

O happy mind, and blessed soul, which deserves to receive thee her Lord God devoutly; and in receiving thee to be filled with spiritual joy!

Oh! how great a Lord does she entertain! how beloved a guest does she bring into her house! how sweet a companion does she receive! how faithful a friend does she accept of! how beautiful and how noble a spouse does she embrace, who deserves to be beloved above all her beloved, and beyond all that she can desire!

Let heaven and earth, with all their attire, be silent in thy presence, O my dearest beloved; for whatever praise or beauty they have, is all the gift of thy bounty; nor can they come up to the beauty of thy name, of whose wisdom there is no number.

CHAPTER IV.
THAT MANY BENEFITS ARE BESTOWED ON THEM WHO COMMUNICATE DEVOUTLY.

The Voice of the Disciple.

1. O Lord, my God, prevent thy servant in the blessings of thy sweetness, that I may approach worthily and devoutly to thy magnificent sacrament.

Raise up my heart towards thee, and deliver me from this heavy sluggishness;

Visit me with thy grace, that I may taste in spirit thy sweetness, which plentifully lies hid in this sacrament as in its fountain;

Illuminate also my eyes to behold so great a mystery, and strengthen me to believe it with an undoubting faith:

For it is thy work, not the power of man; thy sacred institution, not man's invention:

For no man can be found able of himself to comprehend and understand these things, which surpass event subtlety of angels.

What shall I therefore, an unworthy sinner, who am but dust and ashes, be able to search into, or conceive of so high and sacred a mystery?

2. O Lord, in the simplicity of my heart, with a good and firm faith, and in obedience to thy command, I come to thee with hope and reverence; and I do verily believe, that thou art here present in the sacrament, God and man.

It is then thy will that I should receive thee, and through love unite myself to thee.

Wherefore I implore thy mercy; and I beg of thee to give me for this a special grace, that I may be wholly melted away in thee, and overflow with thy love, and seek no more any comfort from any thing else:

For this most high and most excellent sacrament is the health of soul and body, the remedy of all spiritual diseases, by which my vices are cured, my passions are restrained, temptations are overcome or lessened, a greater grace is infused, virtue receives an increase, *Faith* is confirmed, *Hope* strengthened, *Charity* enflamed and enlarged.

3. For thou hast bestowed, and still oftentimes dost bestow, many good things in this sacrament to thy beloved who communicate devoutly, O my God, the support of my soul, who art the repairer of human infirmity, and the giver of all interior comfort:

For thou impartest unto them much consolation, to support them in their many troubles; and thou liftest them up from the depth of their own dejection to the hope of thy protection; and thou dost recreate and enlighten them interiorly with a certain new grace; in such sort, that they who before communion were anxious and felt no affection in them, afterwards being fed with this heavenly meat and drink, find themselves changed for the better.

And thou art better pleased to deal thus with thy elect, to the end that they may truly acknowledge, and plainly experience, how great is their infirmity, when left to themselves, and how much they receive from thy bounty and grace:

For of themselves they are cold, dry, and indevout; but by thee they are made fervent, cheerful, and devout.

For who is he that approaching humbly to the Fountain of Sweetness, does not carry away with him some little sweetness?

Or who, standing by a great fire, does not receive from it some little heat?

Now, thou art a fountain always full, and overflowing; thou art a fire always burning, and never decaying.

4. Wherefore, if I cannot draw out of the fulness of the fountain, nor drink my fill, I will at least set my mouth to the orifice of this heavenly pipe; that so I may draw from thence some small drops to refresh my thirst, to the end that I may not be wholly dried up:

And if I cannot as yet be all heavenly, and all on fire like the cherubim and seraphim, I will, however, endeavour to apply myself to devotion, and to prepare my heart for the acquiring some small flame of divine fire, by the humble receiving of this life-giving sacrament.

And whatever is wanting to me, O good Jesus, most blessed Saviour, do thou in thy bounty and goodness supply for me, who hast vouchsafed to call all unto thee, saying, *Come to me all you that labour, and are burthened, and I will refresh you*. Matthew xi.

5. I *labour* indeed in the sweat of my brow, I am tormented with grief of heart, I am *burthened* with sins, I am troubled with temptations, and am entangled and oppressed with many evil passions; and there is no one to help me, no one to deliver and save me, but thou, O Lord God, my Saviour, to whom I commit myself, and all that is mine, that thou mayest keep me and bring me to everlasting life.

Receive me for the praise and glory of thy name, who hast prepared thy body and blood for my meat and drink.

Grant, O Lord God, my Saviour, that with the frequenting this thy mystery the affection of my devotion may increase.

CHAPTER V.
OF THE DIGNITY OF THE SACRAMENT, AND OF THE PRIESTLY STATE.

The Voice of the Beloved.

1. If thou hast the purity of an angel, and the sanctity of St. John the Baptist, thou wouldst not be worthy to receive or handle this sacrament:

For this is not due to any merits of men, that a man should consecrate and handle the Sacrament of Christ, and receive for his food the bread of angels.

Great is this mystery, and great the dignity of priests, to whom that is given which is not granted to angels:

For priests alone, rightly ordained in the Church, have power to celebrate and consecrate the body of Christ.

The priest indeed is the minister of God, using the word of God, and by the command and institution of God: but God himself is there the principal author and invisible worker, to whom is subject all that he wills, and to whom obeys all that he commands.

2. Thou must therefore give more credit to an omnipotent God, in this most excellent sacrament, than to thy own sense, or any visible sign:

And therefore thou art to approach to this work with fear and reverence.

Take heed to thyself, and see what kind of ministry has been delivered to thee by the imposition of the bishop's hands.

Lo! thou art made a priest, and art consecrated to say Mass: see now that in due time thou faithfully and devoutly offer up sacrifice to God, and that thou behave thyself in such manner as to be without reproof:

Thou hast not lightened thy burthen, but art now bound with a stricter band of discipline, and art obliged to a greater perfection of sanctity.

A priest ought to be adorned with all virtues, and to give example of a good life to others;

His conversation should not be with the vulgar and common ways of men, but with the angels in heaven, or with perfect men upon earth.

3. A priest, clad in his sacred vestments, is Christ's vicegerent, to pray to God for himself, and for all the people, in a suppliant and humble manner:

He has before and behind him the sign of the cross of the Lord, that he may always remember the passion of Christ:

He bears the cross before him in his vestment, that he may diligently behold the footsteps of Christ, and fervently endeavour to follow them:

He is marked with the cross behind, that he may mildly suffer, for God's sake, whatsoever adversities shall befal him from others:

He wears the cross before him, that he may bewail his own sins; and behind him, that, through compassion, he may lament the sins of others, and know that he is placed, as it were, a mediator betwixt God and the sinner:

Neither ought he to cease from prayer and oblation, till he be favoured with the grace and mercy which he implores.

When a priest celebrates, he honours God, he rejoices the angels, he edifies the Church, he helps the living, he obtains rest for the dead, and makes himself partaker of all that is good.

CHAPTER VI.
A PETITION CONCERNING THE EXERCISE PROPER BEFORE COMMUNION.

The Voice of the Disciple.

1. When I consider thy greatness, O Lord, and my own vileness, I tremble very much, and am confounded in myself:

For if I come not to thee, I fly from life; and if I intrude myself unworthily, I incur thy displeasure. What then shall I do, O my God, my helper, my counsellor in necessities?

2. Do thou teach me the right way: appoint me some short exercise proper for the holy communion:

For it is necessary to know in what manner I should reverently and devoutly prepare my heart to thee, for the profitable receiving of thy sacrament, or for celebrating also so great and divine a sacrifice.

CHAPTER VII.
OF THE DISCUSSION OF ONE'S OWN CONSCIENCE, AND OF A RESOLUTION OF AMENDMENT.

The Voice of the Beloved.

1. Above all things it behoves the priest of God to come to the celebrating, handling, and receiving this sacrament, with great humility of heart, and lowly reverence; with an entire faith, and with a pious intention of the honour of God.

Diligently examine thy conscience, and to the best of thy power cleanse and purify it by true contrition and humble confession; so that there be nothing weighty to give thee remorse, and hinder thy free access.

Repent thee of all thy sins in general, and in particular lament and grieve all thy daily offences;

And if thou hast time, confess to God, in the secret of thy heart, all the miseries of thy passions.

2. Sigh and grieve that thou art yet so carnal and worldly; so unmortified in thy passions.

So full of the motions of concupiscence; so unguarded in thy outward senses; so often entangled with many vain imaginations;

So much inclined to exterior things, so negligent as to the interior;

So easy to laughter and dissolution; so hard to tears and compunction.

So prone to relaxation, and to the pleasures of the flesh; so sluggish to austerity and fervour;

So curious to hear news, and to see fine sights; so remiss to embrace things humble and abject;

So covetous to possess much; so sparing in giving; so close in retaining;

So inconsiderate in speech; so little able to hold thy peace;

So disorderly in thy carriage; so over eager in thy actions;

So greedy at meat; so deaf to the word of God;

So hasty for rest; so slow to labour;

So wakeful to hear idle tales; so drowsy to watch in the service of God;

So hasty to make an end of thy prayer; so wandering as to attention.

So negligent in saying thy office; so tepid in celebrating; so dry at the time of receiving;

So quickly distracted; so seldom quite recollected within thyself;

So easily moved to anger; so apt to take offence at others;

So prone to judge; so severe in reprehending;

So joyful in prosperity; so weak in adversity.

So often proposing many good things, and effecting little.

3. Having confessed and bewailed these, and other thy defects, with sorrow and great dislike of thy own weakness, make a strong resolution always to amend thy life, and to advance in virtue.

Then with a full resignation, and with thy whole will, offer thyself up to the honour of my name, on the altar of thy heart, as a perpetual holocaust, by committing faithfully to me both thy soul and body;

That so thou mayest be able to approach to offer up sacrifice to God, and to receive for thy salvation the sacrament of my body.

4. For there is no oblation more worthy, nor satisfaction greater, for the washing away of sins, than to offer up one's self purely and entirely to God, together with the oblation of the body of Christ, in the Mass and in the communion.

If a man does what lies in him, and is truly penitent; as often as he shall come to me for pardon and grace; as I live, saith the Lord, who will not the death of a sinner, but rather that he should be converted and live; I will no longer remember his sins, but all shall be forgiven him. Ezekiel xviii.

CHAPTER VIII.
OF THE OBLATION OF CHRIST ON THE CROSS, AND OF THE RESIGNATION OF OURSELVES.

The Voice of the Beloved.

1. As I willingly offered myself to God, my Father, for thy sins, with my hands stretched out upon the cross, and my body naked, so that nothing remained in me which was not turned into a sacrifice, for to appease the divine wrath;

Even so must thou willingly offer thyself to me daily in the Mass, for a pure and holy oblation, together with all thy powers and affections, as heartily as thou art able.

What do I require more of thee, than that thou endeavour to resign thyself entirely to me?

Whatsoever thou givest besides thyself, I regard not; for I seek not thy gift, but thyself.

2. As it would not suffice thee, if thou hadst all things but me; so neither can it please me, whatever thou givest, as long as thou offerest not thyself.

Offer thyself to me, and give thy whole self for God, and thy offering will be accepted.

Behold, I offered my whole self to the Father for thee, and have given my whole body and blood for thy food, that I might be all thine, and thou mightest be always mine:

But if thou wilt stand upon thy own bottom, and wilt not offer thyself freely to my will, thy offering is not perfect, nor will there be an entire union betwixt us.

Therefore, before all thy works, thou must make a free oblation of thyself into the hands of God, if thou desire to obtain liberty and grace:

For the reason why so few become illuminated and internally free, is because they do not wholly renounce themselves.

My sentence stands firm. Unless a man renounce all, he cannot be my disciple. Luke xiv.

If therefore thou desirest to be my disciple, offer up thyself to me with all thy affections.

CHAPTER IX.
THAT WE MUST OFFER OURSELVES, AND ALL THAT IS OURS, TO GOD, AND PRAY FOR ALL.

The Voice of the Disciple.

1. Lord, all things are thine that are in heaven and earth.

I desire to offer up myself to thee as a voluntary oblation, and to remain for ever thine.

Lord, in the sincerity of my heart, I offer myself to thee this day, to be thy servant evermore, to serve thee, and to become a sacrifice of perpetual praise to thee.

Receive me with this sacred oblation of thy precious body, which I offer to thee this day in the presence of thy angels invisibly standing by, that it may be for mine and all the people's salvation.

2. Lord, I offer to thee all my sins and offences, which I have committed in thy sight and that of thy holy angels, from the day that I was first capable of sin until this hour, upon thy propitiatory altar, that thou mayest burn and consume them all with the fire of thy charity, and mayest remove all the stains of my sins, and cleanse my conscience from all offences, and restore to me thy grace, which I have lost by sin, by fully pardoning me all, and mercifully receiving me to the kiss of peace.

3. What can I do for my sins, but humbly confess them, and lament them, and incessantly implore thy mercy for them?

Hear me, I beseech thee, in thy mercy, where I stand before thee, O my God:

All my sins displease me exceedingly; I will never commit them any more: I am sorry for them, and will be sorry for them as long as I live; I am willing to do penance for them, and to make satisfaction to the utmost of my power.

Forgive, O my God, forgive me my sins, for thy holy name's sake: save my soul, which thou hast redeemed with thy precious blood.

Behold I commit myself to thy mercy, I resign myself into thy hands.

Deal with me according to thy goodness, not according to my wickedness and iniquity.

4. I offer also to thee all the good I have, though very little and imperfect: that thou mayest make it better and sanctify it; that thou mayest be pleased with it, and make it acceptable to thee, and perfect it more and more; and mayest, moreover, bring me, who am a slothful and unprofitable wretch, to a good and happy end.

5 I offer also to thee all the godly desires of thy devout servants; the necessities of my parents, friends, brethren, sisters, and of all those that are dear to me; and of all such, as for the love of thee have been benefactors to me or others; or who have desired and begged of me to offer up prayers and masses for themselves and all that belonged to them; whether they live as yet in the flesh, or whether they are now departed out of this world;

That they all may be sensible of the assistance of thy grace, of the benefit of thy comfort, of thy protection from all dangers, and of a deliverance from their pains; and that being freed from all evils, they may with joy give worthy thanks to thee.

6. I offer up also to thee my prayers, and this sacrifice of propitiation for them in particular, who have in any thing wronged me, grieved me or abused me, or have done me any damage or displeasure;

And for all those likewise whom I have at any time grieved, troubled, injured, or scandalized, by word or deed, knowingly or unknowingly; that it may please thee to forgive us all our sins and offences one against another.

Take, O Lord, from our hearts all jealousy, indignation, wrath and contention, and whatsoever may hurt charity, and lessen brotherly love.

Have mercy, O Lord, have mercy on those that crave thy mercy; give grace to them that stand in need thereof; and grant that we may be worthy to enjoy thy grace, and that we may attain to life everlasting. **Amen.**

CHAPTER X.
THAT THE HOLY COMMUNION IS NOT LIGHTLY TO BE FORBORNE.

The Voice of the Beloved.

1. Thou oughtest often to have recourse to the fountain of Grace, and of Divine Mercy; to the Fountain of all Goodness and Purity; that thou mayest be healed of thy passions and vices, and be made more strong and vigilant against all the temptations and deceits of the devil.

The enemy, knowing the very great advantage and remedy which is in the holy communion, strives by all means and occasions, as much as he is able, to withdraw and hinder faithful and devout persons from it.

2. For when some are preparing themselves for the sacred communion, they suffer the greater assault of Satan.

This wicked spirit, as it is written in Job, cometh among the sons of God to trouble them with his accustomed malice, or to make them ever fearful and perplexed, that so he may diminish their devotion, or by his assaults take away their faith: it haply they may altogether forbear the communion, or at least approach to it with tepidity.

But there is no heed to be taken of his wiles, and suggestions, be they never so filthy and abominable; but all his attempts art to be turned back upon his own head.

The wretch is to be contemned and scorned, nor is the holy communion to be omitted for his assaults, and the commotions which he causeth.

3. Oftentimes also a person is hindered by too great solicitude for obtaining devotion, and a certain anxiety about making his confession.

Follow herein the counsel of the wise, and put away all anxiety and scruple; for it hindereth the grace of God, and destroyeth devotion.

Leave not the holy communion for every small trouble or vexation, but go quickly to confession, and willingly forgive others their offences against thee.

And if thou hast offended any one, humbly crave pardon, and God will readily forgive thee.

4. What doth it avail to delay thy confession for a long time, or to put off the holy communion?

Purge thyself with speed, spit out the venom presently, make haste to take this *remedy*, and thou shalt find it to be better with thee, than if thou hadst deferred it for a long time.

If thou lettest it alone to-day for this cause, perhaps to-morrow a greater will fall out, and so thou mayest be hindered a long time from communion, and become more unfit:

With all possible speed shake off this heaviness and sloth, for it is to no purpose to continue long in disquiet, to pass a long time in trouble, and for these daily impediments to withdraw thyself from the *divine mysteries*.

Yea, it is very hurtful to defer the communion long; for this usually causeth a great lukewarmness and numbness.

Alas! some tepid and dissolute people are willing to put off their confession, and desire that their communion should be deferred, lest they should be obliged thereby to keep a stricter watch over themselves.

5 Ah! how little is their love of God, how weak is their devotion who so easily put by the sacred communion?

How happy is he, and acceptable to God, who so liveth, and keepeth his conscience in such purity, as to be ready and well disposed to communicate every day, if it were permitted, and he might do it without note.

If sometimes a person abstains out of humility, or by reason of some lawful impediment, he is to be commended for his reverence.

But if sloth steal upon him, he must stir up himself, and do what lieth in him; and God will assist his desire, for his good will, which he chiefly regards.

6. And when he is lawfully hindered, he must yet always have a good will and a pious intention to communicate, and so he shall not lose the fruit of the sacrament.

For every devout man may every day and hour receive Christ spiritually without any prohibition, and with profit to his soul.

And yet on certain days, and at the time appointed, he ought to receive sacramentally with an affectionate reverence the body of his Redeemer, and rather aim at the honour of God, than seek his own comfort.

For he communicates mystically, and is invisibly fed, as often as he devoutly calleth to mind the mystery of the incarnation of Christ, and his passion; and is inflamed with the love of him.

7. He that prepareth not himself, but when a festival draweth near, or when custom compelleth him thereunto, shall often be unprepared.

Blessed is he that offereth himself up as an holocaust to the Lord, as often as he celebrates or communicates.

Be neither too long, nor too hasty in celebrating, but observe the good common manner of those with whom thou livest.

Thou oughtest not to be tedious and troublesome to others, but to keep the common way, according to the appointment of superiors; and rather suit thyself to the profit of others, than to thine own devotion or affection.

CHAPTER XI.
THAT THE BODY OF CHRIST AND THE HOLY SCRIPTURE ARE MOST NECESSARY TO A FAITHFUL SOUL.

The Voice of the Disciple.

1. O Sweetest Lord Jesus, how great sweetness hath a devout soul that feasteth with thee in thy banquet; where there is no other meat set before her to be eaten but thyself her only beloved, and most to be desired above all the desires of her heart!

And to me indeed it would be delightful to pour out tears in thy presence, with the whole affection of my heart, and like the devout Magdalen to wash thy feet with my tears.

But where is this devotion? Where is this so plentiful shedding of holy tears?

Surely in the sight of thee, and of thy holy angels, my whole heart ought to be inflamed, and to weep for joy.

For I have thee in the sacrament truly present, though hidden under another form.

2. For to behold thee in thine own divine brightness, is what my eyes would not be able to endure, neither could the whole world subsist in the splendour of the glory of thy Majesty.

In this therefore thou condescendest to my weakness, that thou hidest thyself under the sacrament.

I truly have and adore him whom the angels adore in heaven; but I as yet in *faith*, they by *sight* and without a veil.

I must be content with the light of *true faith*, and walk therein till the day of eternal brightness break forth, and the shades of figures pass away.

But when that which is perfect shall come, the use of the sacraments shall cease: for the blessed in heavenly glory stand not in need of the remedy of the sacraments.

For they rejoice without end in the presence of God, beholding his glory face to face; and being transformed from glory into the glory of the incomprehensible Deity, they taste the *Word of God made flesh*, as he was from the beginning, and as he remaineth for ever.

3. When I call to mind these wonders, even every spiritual comfort becomes grievously tedious to me; because as long as I behold not my Lord openly in his glory, I make no account of whatsoever I see and hear in the world.

Thou art my witness, O God, that not one thing can comfort me, nor any thing created give me rest, but only thou, my God, whom I desire for ever to contemplate.

But this is not possible whilst I remain in this mortal life.

And therefore I must frame myself to much patience, and submit myself to thee in all my desires.

For thy saints also, O Lord, who now rejoice with thee in the Kingdom of heaven, whilst they were living, expected in faith and great patience the coming of thy glory. What they believed, I believe; what they hoped for, I hope for; and whether they are come, I trust that I also through thy grace shall come.

In the mean time I will walk in faith, strengthened by the example of thy saints.

I shall have moreover for my comfort, and the direction of my life, thy holy books; and above all these things, thy most holy body for a singular remedy and refuge.

4. For in this life I find there are two things especially necessary for me, without which this miserable life would be insupportable.

Whilst I am kept in the prison of this body, I acknowledge myself to need two things, to wit, *food* and *light*.

Thou hast therefore given to me, weak as I am, thy sacred body for the nourishment of my soul and body, and thou hast set *thy Word as a light to my feet*. Psalms cxviii.

Without these two I could not well live, for the Word of God is the light of my soul, and thy sacrament is *the bread of Life*.

These also may be called the two tables set on the one side, and on the other, in the store house of the *holy church*.

One is the table of the *holy altar*, having the *holy bread*, that is the precious *Body of Christ*.

The other is that of the *divine law*, containing *holy doctrine*, teaching the *right faith*, and firmly leading even within the *veil*, where are the *holies of holies*:

Thanks be to thee, O Lord Jesus, Light of eternal Light, for the table of *holy doctrine* which thou hast afforded us by the ministry of thy servants, the prophets and apostles, and other teachers.

5. Thanks be to thee, O thou Creator and Redeemer of men, who, to manifest thy love to the whole world, hast prepared a great supper, wherein thou hast set before us to be eaten, not the typical lamb, but thy most sacred body and blood: rejoicing all the faithful with thy holy banquet, and replenishing them with the cup of salvation, in which are all the delights of paradise; and the holy angels do feast with us, but with a more happy sweetness.

6. O how great and honourable is the office of priests, to whom it is given to consecrate with sacred words the Lord of Majesty; to bless *him* with their lips, to hold *him* with their hands, to receive *him* with their own mouth, and to administer *him* to others!

Oh! how clean ought those hands to be, how pure that mouth, how holy that body, how unspotted the heart of a *priest*, into whom thou the Author of Purity so often enters!

From the mouth of a *priest* nothing but what is *holy*, no word but what is *good* and *profitable* ought to proceed, who so often receives the sacrament of Christ.

7. His eyes ought to be *simple*, and *chaste*, which are used to behold the *Body of Christ;* his hands *pure* and lifted up to heaven, which use to handle the Creator of heaven and earth.

Unto the priest especially it is said in the law, *Be you holy, for I the Lord your God am holy*. Leviticus xix. 20.

8. Let thy grace, O Almighty God, assist us, that we, who have undertaken the office of priesthood, may serve thee worthily and devoutly in all purity and good conscience.

And if we cannot live in so great innocency as we ought, grant us at least duly to bewail the sins which we have committed; and in the spirit of humility, and the resolution of a good-will, to serve thee more fervently for the time to come.

CHAPTER XII.
THAT HE WHO IS TO COMMUNICATE OUGHT TO PREPARE HIMSELF FOR CHRIST WITH GREAT DILIGENCE.

The Voice of the Beloved.

1. I Am the lover of purity, and the giver of all holiness.

I seek a pure heart, and there is the place of my *rest*.

Make ready for me a large upper room furnished, and I will make the pasch with thee, together with my disciples. Mark xiv. Luke xxii.

If thou wilt have me come to thee, and remain with thee; purge out the old leaven, and make clean the habitation of thy heart;

Shut out the whole world, and all the tumult of vices; sit like a sparrow solitary on the house top, and think of thy excesses in the bitterness of thy soul.

For every lover prepareth the best and fairest room for his dearly beloved; and hereby is known the affection of him that entertaineth his beloved.

2. Know nevertheless, that thou canst not sufficiently prepare thyself by the merit of any action of thine, although thou shouldst prepare thyself a whole year together, and think of nothing else.

But it is of my mere goodness and grace that thou art suffered to come to my table; as if a beggar should be invited to dinner by a rich man, who hath nothing else to return him for his benefit, but to humble himself, and to give him thanks.

Do what lieth in thee, and do it diligently; not for custom, nor for necessity; but with fear, and reverence, and affection, receive the body of thy beloved Lord, thy God, who vouchsafeth to come to thee.

I am he that have invited thee, I have commanded it to be done, I will supply what is wanting in thee, come and receive me.

3. When I bestow the grace of devotion give thanks to thy God, not for that thou art worthy, but because I have had mercy on thee.

If thou hast it not, but rather findest thyself dry, continue in prayer, sigh and knock, and give not over, till thou receivest some crum or drop of saving grace.

Thou hast need of me, not I of thee.

Neither dost thou come to sanctify me, but I come to sanctify and make thee better;

Thou comest that thou mayest be sanctified by me, and united to me; that thou mayest receive new grace, and be inflamed anew to amendment.

Neglect not this grace, but prepare thy heart with all diligence, and bring thy beloved into thee.

4. But thou oughtest not only to prepare thyself to devotion before communion, but carefully also to keep thyself therein after receiving the sacrament; neither is the carefully guarding of thyself afterwards less required than the devoutly preparing thyself before: for a good guard afterwards is the best preparation again for the obtaining of greater grace.

For what renders a man very much indisposed is, if he presently pour himself out upon exterior comforts.

Beware of much talk, remain in secret, and enjoy thy God; for thou hast him whom all the world cannot take from thee.

I am he to whom thou oughtest to give thy whole self; so that thou mayest henceforward live, without all solicitude, not in thyself, but in me.

CHAPTER XIII.
THAT A DEVOUT SOUL OUGHT TO DESIRE WITH HER WHOLE HEART TO BE UNITED TO CHRIST IN THE SACRAMENT.

The Voice of the Disciple.

1. Who will give me, O Lord, to find thee alone, that I may open my whole heart to thee, and enjoy thee as my soul desireth; and that no one may now despise me, nor any thing created move me or regard me; but thou alone mayest speak to me, and I to thee; as the **Beloved** is wont to speak to his **Beloved**, and a friend to banquet with his friend.

This I pray for, this I desire, that I may be wholly united to thee, and may withdraw my heart from all created things; and by the holy communion, and often celebrating, may more and more learn to relish heavenly and eternal things.

Ah! Lord God, when shall I be wholly united to thee, and absorpt in thee, and altogether forgetful of myself:

Thou in me, and I in thee; and so grant us both to continue in one.

2. Verily thou art my **Beloved**, the choicest amongst thousands, in whom my soul is well pleased to dwell all the days of her life:

Verily, thou art my **peace-maker**, in whom is sovereign **peace** and true **rest;** out of whom is **labour** and **sorrow**, and endless **misery:**

Thou art in truth, a hidden God, and thy counsel is not with the wicked; but thy conversation is with the humble and the simple.

Oh! how sweet is thy spirit, O Lord, who, to shew thy sweetness towards thy children, vouchsafest to feed them with the most delicious bread which cometh down from heaven!

Surely, there is no other nation so great, that hath their God so nigh to them, as thou our God art present to all thy faithful; to whom, for their daily comfort, and for the raising up their hearts to heaven, thou gavest thyself to be eaten and enjoyed.

3. For what other nation is there so honoured as the Christian people!

Or what creature under heaven so beloved as a devout soul, into whom God cometh, that he may feed her with his glorious flesh?

Oh! unspeakable grace! Oh! wonderful condescension! Oh! infinite love, singularly bestowed upon man!

But what return shall I make to the Lord for this grace, and for so extraordinary a charity?

There is nothing that I can give him that will please him better, than if I give up my heart entirely to God, and unite it closely to him.

Then all that is within me shall rejoice exceedingly, when my soul shall be perfectly united to my God:

Then will he say to me, If thou wilt be with me, I will be with thee; and I will answer him: Vouchsafe, O Lord, to remain with me, and I will willingly be with thee.

This is my whole desire, that my heart may be united to thee.

CHAPTER XIV.
OF THE ARDENT DESIRE OF SOME DEVOUT PERSONS TO RECEIVE THE BODY OF CHRIST.

The Voice of the Disciple.

1. Oh! how great is the abundance of thy sweetness, O Lord, which thou hast laid up for them that fear thee. Psalms xxx.

When I remember some devout persons, who come to thy sacrament with the greatest devotion and affection, I am often confounded and ashamed within myself, that I approach so tepidly and coldly to thy altar, and to the table of the holy communion;

That I remain so dry, and without affection of heart; that I am not wholly set on fire in thy presence, O my God; nor so earnestly drawn and affected, as many devout persons have been, who, out of a vehement desire of communion, and a sensible love in their hearts, could not contain themselves from weeping;

But with their whole souls eagerly thirsted to approach, both with the mouth of their heart and of their body, to thee, O God, the living Fountain; being in no wise able to moderate or satisfy their hunger, but by receiving thy body with all joy and spiritual greediness.

2. Oh! **true ardent faith** of these persons, being a probable argument of thy sacred presence!

For they truly know their Lord in the breaking of bread, whose heart burneth so mightily within them, from Jesus his walking with them. **Luke** xxiv.

Such affection and devotion as this, so vehement a love and burning, is often far from me.

Be thou merciful to me, O good Jesus, sweet and gracious Lord; and grant me, thy poor beggar, to feel, sometimes at least, in the sacred communion, some little of the cordial affection of thy love, that my *faith* may be more strengthened, my *hope* in thy goodness increased, and that my *charity*, being once perfectly enkindled, and having tasted the *Manna* of heaven, may never decay.

3. Moreover, thy mercy is able to give me the grace I desire, and to visit me in thy great clemency with the spirit of fervour, when it shall please thee:

For though I burn not at present with so great a desire as those that are so singularly devoted to thee; yet, by thy grace, I desire to have this same great inflamed desire; praying and wishing that I may be made partaker with all such thy fervent lovers, and be numbered in their holy company.

CHAPTER XV.
THAT THE GRACE OF DEVOTION IS OBTAINED BY HUMILITY AND SELF-DENIAL.

1. Thou oughtest to seek the grace of devotion earnestly, to ask it fervently, to wait for it patiently and confidently, to receive it thankfully, to keep it humbly, to work with it diligently, and to commit to God the time and manner of this heavenly visitation, until it shall please him to come unto thee.

Thou oughtest chiefly to humble thyself, when thou feelest inwardly little or no devotion; and yet not to be too much dejected, nor to grieve inordinately.

God often giveth, in one short moment, what he hath a long time denied:

He giveth sometimes in the end, that which in the beginning of prayer he deferred to grant.

2. If grace were always presently given, and ever at hand with a wish, it would be more than man's infirmity could well bear:

Therefore the **grace of devotion** is to be expected with a good hope and humble patience. Yet impute it to thyself, and to thy sins, when it is not given to thee, or when it is secretly taken away.

It is sometimes a little thing that hinders or hides grace from us; if that may be called **little**, and not rather **great**, which hindereth so great a good:

But if thou remove this same, be it small or great, and perfectly overcome it, thou shalt have thy desire.

3. For as soon as ever thou hast delivered thyself up to God with thy whole heart, and neither seekest this nor that for thine own pleasure or will, but wholly placest thyself in him, thou shalt find thyself united and at peace; for nothing will relish so well, and please thee so much, as the good pleasure of the divine will.

Whosoever therefore with a single heart shall direct his attention upwards to God, and purge himself of all inordinate love or dislike of any created thing, he shall be the most fit to receive grace, and worthy of the gift of devotion:

For the Lord bestows his blessing there where he finds the vessels empty.

And the more perfectly one forsakes these things below, and the more he dies to himself by the contempt of himself, the more speedily grace cometh, entereth in more plentifully, and the higher it elevateth the free heart.

4. **Then shall he see and abound, he shall admire, and his heart shall be enlarged** within him, because the hand of the Lord is with him, and he has put himself wholly into his **hand** for ever. Behold, thus shall the man be blessed that seeketh God with his whole heart, and taketh not his soul in vain.

Such a one as this, in receiving the Holy Eucharist, obtains a great grace of **divine union;** because he looks not towards his own devotion and comfort, but, above all devotion and comfort, regards the honour and glory of God.

CHAPTER XVI.
THAT WE OUGHT TO LAY OPEN OUR NECESSITIES TO CHRIST, AND CRAVE HIS GRACE.

The Voice of the Disciple.

1. O Most sweet and loving Lord, whom I now desire to receive with all devotion, thou knowest my weakness, and the necessity which I endure; in how great evils and vices I am immersed; now often I am oppressed, tempted, troubled, and defiled;

To thee I come for remedy; I pray to thee for comfort and succour.

I speak to him that knows all things, to whom all that is within me is manifest, and who alone can perfectly comfort and help me.

Thou knowest what good I stand most inn need of, and how poor I am in virtues.

2. Behold, I stand before thee poor and naked, begging thy grace, and imploring thy mercy:

Feed thy hungry beggar; inflame my coldness with the fire of thy love; enlighten my blindness with the brightness of thy presence;

Turn all earthly things to me into bitterness; all things grievous and cross into patience; all things below and created, into contempt and oblivion:

Lift up my heart to thee in heaven, and suffer me not to wander upon earth:

Be thou only sweet to me from henceforth for evermore; for thou only art my meat and my drink, my love and my joy, my sweetness and all my good.

3. Oh! that with thy presence thou wouldst inflame, burn, and transform me into thyself, that I may be made one spirit with thee, by the grace of internal union, and by the melting of ardent love!

Suffer me not to go from thee hungry and dry; but deal with me in thy mercy, as thou hast dealt wonderfully with thy saints.

What marvel if I should be wholly set on fire by thee, and should die to myself; since thou art a **fire** always burning, and never decaying; a *love* purifying the heart, and enlightening the understanding.

CHAPTER XVII.
OF FERVENT LOVE AND VEHEMENT DESIRE TO RECEIVE CHRIST.

The Voice of the Disciple.

1. With the greatest devotion and burning love, with all the affection and fervour of my heart, I desire to receive thee, O Lord; as many saints and devout persons, who were most pleasing to thee in holiness of life, and most fervent in devotion, have desired thee when they have communicated.

O my God, my eternal love, my whole good, and never-ending happiness, I would gladly receive thee with the most vehement desire, and most worthy reverence, that any of the saints ever had or could feel.

2. And though I be unworthy to have all those feelings of devotion, yet I offer to thee the whole affection of my heart, as if I alone had all those highly pleasing inflamed desires;

Yea, and whatsoever a godly mind can conceive and desire, all this, with the greatest reverence and most inward affection, I offer and present to thee:

I desire to reserve nothing to myself, but freely and most willingly to sacrifice myself, and all that is mine, to thee.

O Lord, my God, my Creator and Redeemer, I desire to receive thee this day with such **affection, reverence, praise**, and **honour;** with such **gratitude, worthiness,** and **love;** with such **faith, hope,** and **purity,** as thy most holy Mother, the glorious Virgin Mary, received and desired thee, when she humbly and devoutly answered the angel, who declared to her the mystery of the incarnation; **Behold the handmaid of the Lord, let it be done unto me according to thy word**. Luke i.

3. And as thy blessed forerunner, the most excellent among the saints, John the Baptist, in thy presence leaped for joy through the Holy Ghost, whilst he was as yet shut up in his mother's womb; and afterwards seeing Jesus walking amongst men, humbling himself exceedingly, said with devout affection, **The friend of the bridegroom that standeth and heareth him, and rejoiceth with joy for the voice of the bridegroom.** John iii. So I also wish to be inflamed with great and holy desires, and to present myself to thee with my whole heart:

Wherefore I here offer and present myself to thee the excessive joys of all devout hearts, their ardent affections, their extasies and supernatural illuminations, and heavenly visions; together with all the virtues and praises which are or shall be celebrated by all creatures in heaven and earth; for myself and all such as are recommended to my prayers, that by all thou mayest be worthily praised and glorified for ever.

4. Receive my wishes, O Lord, my God, and my desire of giving thee infinite praise and immense blessing, which, according to the multitude of thy unspeakable greatness, are most justly due to thee.

These I render, and desire to render to thee every day and every moment: and I invite and entreat all the heavenly spirits, and all thy faithful, with my prayers and affections, to join with me in giving thee praises and thanks.

5. Let all people, tribes, and tongues praise thee, and magnify thy holy and sweet name, with the highest jubilation and ardent devotion.

And let all who reverently and devoutly celebrate thy most high sacrament, and receive it with full faith, find grace and mercy at thy hands, and humbly pray for me, a sinful creature.

And when they shall have obtained their desired devotion and joyful union, and shall depart from thy sacred heavenly table, well comforted, and wonderfully nourished, let them vouchsafe to remember my poor soul.

CHAPTER XVIII.
THAT A MAN BE NOT A CURIOUS SEARCHER INTO THIS SACRAMENT, BUT A FOLLOWER OF CHRIST, SUBMITTING HIS SENSE TO HOLY FAITH.

The Voice of the Beloved.

1. Thou must, beware of curious and unprofitable searching into this most profound sacrament, if thou wilt not sink into the depth of doubt.

He that is a searcher of Majesty shall be oppressed by glory. Proverbs xxv. God is able to work more than man can understand.

A pious and humble inquiry after **truth** is tolerable, which is always ready to be taught, and studies to walk in the sound doctrine of the **Fathers**.

2. Blessed is that simplicity that leaveth the difficult ways of disputes, and goeth on in the plain and sure path of God's commandments.

Many have lost devotion, whilst they would search into high things.

It is **faith** that is required of thee, and a **sincere life;** not the height of understanding, not diving deep into the mysteries of God.

If thou dost not understand nor comprehend those things that are under thee, how shouldst thou comprehend those things that are above thee?

Submit thyself to God, and humble thy **sense** to **faith**, and the light of knowledge shall be given thee, as far as shall be profitable and necessary for thee.

3. Some are grievously tempted about faith and the sacrament; but this is not to be imputed to them, but rather to the enemy.

Be not thou anxious, stand not to dispute with thy thoughts, nor to answer the doubts which the devil suggests, but believe the words of God, believe his saints and prophets, and the wicked enemy will fly from thee.

It is often very profitable to the servant of God to suffer such things;

For the devil tempteth not unbelievers and sinners, whom he already securely possesseth; but the faithful and devout he many ways tempteth and molesteth.

4. Go forward therefore with a sincere and undoubted faith, and with an humble reverence approach to this sacrament; and whatsoever thou art not able to understand, commit securely to God, who is **Omnipotent**.

God never deceiveth, but he is deceived that trusts too much to himself:

God walketh with the simple, and revealeth himself to the humble; he giveth understanding to little ones, openeth the gate of knowledge to pure minds, and hideth his grace from the curious and proud.

Human **reason** is weak and may be deceived; but true **faith** cannot be deceived.

5. All reason and natural search ought to follow faith, and not to go before it, nor oppose it;

For **faith** and **love** are here predominant, and work by hidden ways in this most holy and super-excellent sacrament.

God, who is eternal and incomprehensible, and of infinite power, doth great and inscrutable things in heaven and earth, and there is no searching out his wonderful works.

If the works of God were such as might be easily comprehended by human reason, they could not be called wonderful and unspeakable.

The End.

Made in the USA
Middletown, DE
27 March 2021

36406951R00111